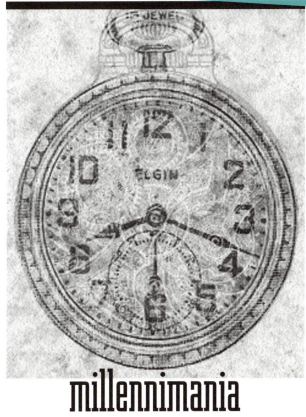

# millennimania

written by

# MARTIN WEBER

Ministerial Association
General Conference of Seventh-day Adventists

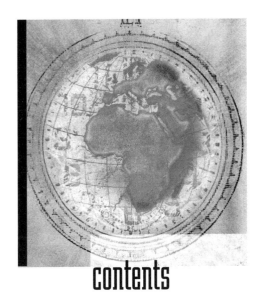

# contents

# Chapter one
## THE PARTY'S OVER

Hurry! Put the kids to bed before the 6:00 news comes on. It's about sex, lies, and audio tapes–from the White House. A designing young intern has infiltrated the Oval Office, which becomes a playpen for presidential passions. The world is mesmerized as lurid details seep out. The first lady stands by her man, denying everything, the stalwart feminist now looking like a classic enabler. Then the blue dress emerges from the FBI lab with the sin-stained evidence, and the leadership of the free world trembles in the balance. The House of Representatives votes to impeach.

Who needs a soap opera? No scriptwriter could invent a story line sleazier than this stuff.

Unprecedented! Not that presidential peccadillos are anything new, but at least FDR and even JFK managed to maintain the dignity of the office. After all, the successors of Abraham Lincoln were supposedly the moral leaders of the nation. How times have changed! Can it be that just three presidential campaigns ago, Gary Hart felt forced to resign in disgrace after his "monkey business" with Donna Rice?

Now, however, "the unrighteous know no shame" (Zephaniah 3:5). In fact, the president proclaimed himself honored for the opportunity to defend the U.S. Constitution from partisan attacks of political enemies determined to distract him from the work the American people had elected him to do.

Perhaps most distressing of all, Bill Clinton is America's most fervently religious chief executive since the devout Jimmy Carter. Wagging his finger in righteous indignation, the president declared that he never had done anything inappropriate with "that woman, Monica Lewinski." No way. Why he never even was alone with her! Not to his best recollection, anyway. If you can believe that story, then he who once smoked marijuana but didn't inhale now managed to unzip without having sex and then lie under oath without perjuring himself. All this from the one who had promised to provide the most ethical administration in the history of American government.

Not that the Republican political opposition was worthy of casting stones. When porno peddler Larry Flynt showed up in Washington waving a million dollars for anyone with a story to tell and the shamelessness to go with it, both houses of Congress shuddered. Too many lawmakers were doing business on the side with former cherry blossom queens imported from their districts to run their Washington offices during the day and run around town with them at night. Meanwhile back home, unsuspecting wives raised their all-American families, and everybody made sure to be seen at church on Sundays.

Flynt became the self-appointed counterpart to Kenneth Starr. Not only was the notorious pornographer far more popular in public opinion polls than the independent prosecutor, but he also managed to force an enemy out of elected office. He snagged no less than Speaker-elect of the House of Representatives Bob Livingston, an unsparing critic of presidential immorality. Already silver-haired Henry Hyde, perhaps the most respected Congressman, had to own up to "youthful indiscretions" committed as a public servant in his 40's. Evidently Capitol Hill offered little high ground for some moral campaigners demanding the impeachment of the president.

But the American people didn't want their president impeached, anyway. As the scandal plunged to new depths, eventually with rape allegations deemed credible by the president of NBC News, Bill Clinton's polls soared to new heights. How come? "Because from the least of them even to the greatest of them, everyone is given to covetousness" (Jeremiah 6:13). Remember that 1992 presidential campaign slogan, which summarized the spirit of America: "It's the economy, stupid!" So why care now about "bimbo eruptions" or whatever else might have happened with Paula Jones, so long as Dow Jones keeps moving us onward and upward?

Character doesn't count. Well, maybe for investment counselors managing our money or overcharging plumbers fixing our toilets, but not for the president leading our nation.

## TRIUMPH OF THE '60S

Back during Christ's time on earth, King Herod had an adulterous affair that scandalized the nation. John the Baptist boldly confronted him. "Herod wanted to kill John, but he was afraid of the people, because they considered him a prophet" (Matthew 14:5). These days, Herod would have little to fear from the American people. Confronted with his immorality, Herod could hold a press conference blasting his accuser for invading his family's privacy and diverting his energies from leading the nation. And no doubt Herod's popular ratings would soar. All in the name of tolerance.

Such is the state of moral affairs in the United States and many other nations today. Why blame our elected politicians when they simply reflect our own sunken standards? Who can deny that the Western world has been plummeting in a moral free fall since the '60s? Exhibit A would be our media, which reflect cultural values. Back In the '50s, movies showed respect for God, Jesus, and the Bible. Witness the blockbusters Ten Commandments, King of Kings and Ben Hur. Even secular movies cultivated a measure of modesty and morality. Hollywood kept its clothes on in front of cameras. Movie stars who manifested immorality risked their careers. Recall how Ingrid Bergman's film career soured after her extra-marital adventures hit the news.

With the dawning of the '60s, music for the most part remained comparatively harmless. Sure, Elvis shook his pelvis, but television showed only his tamer torso. One big hit talked about going to the chapel and getting married. The Beach Boys concurred: "Wouldn't it be nice if we got married." The Beatles chimed in with "I Want to Hold Your Hand."

If only that was all John Lennon had wanted to do. Soon he was leading the plunge into psychedelic sin, determined to revolutionize society without reference to God. "Give peace a chance," he preached. Yet an unrelenting restlessness ravaged his own life. "All you need is love," he sang. Yet he struggled to show affection to his own son. "Drugs will set you free," Lennon promised by making his albums a thinly-veiled sales pitch for LSD, heroin and marijuana. Yet chemical addiction enslaved his own body, mind and soul with bonds he couldn't break.

Nevertheless, Lennon became perhaps the premier apostle of a revolution that ultimately undermined Western society. Timothy Leary joined in, urging students to "turn on, tune in, drop out." Sex, drugs and rock and roll, seasoned with Eastern mysticism, replaced Christian principles and influence in this dawning of the Age of Aquarius.

Make love, not war! Do your own thing. Power to the people! Don't trust anyone over thirty.

Peaceful college campuses suffered chaotic sit-ins, led by scruffy radicals who rousted gray-haired administrators from their offices. Teach-ins proclaimed the new gospel of situation ethics: no more moral absolutes. The permissive Dr. Spock supplanted biblical Proverbs with his own textbook for child-raising. Time magazine actually raised the question on its cover: "Is God Dead?" To the Woodstock generation, even if He still had a pulse, He wasn't relevant.

Not that everything about the '60s was negative. The civil rights movement finally kicked into high gear after three centuries of racial oppression. Today, Anglos as well as African-Americans can thank God that Martin Luther King's dream was non-violent, or our cities might have gone up in flames. Finally African-American students gained equal access to a college education. Imagine!

But now, many youth of the inner cities spurn the opportunities for which their parents and grandparents had suffered beatings and imprisonment. They tend to ridicule their peers who do their homework and plan to attend college for academics rather than athletics. Hopelessness reigns. Urine-stained alleys littered with needles and crack vials echo with music promoting violence, narcotics and cheap sex. As coroners lose track of body counts, record company executives gleefully chart profits in corporate boardrooms. Most of these dark-suited men with blood-stained hands have white faces. Their callous cannibalization of anguished ghetto youth is one example of how racism still slithers throughout American society.

Also, many state governments fortify their budgets by saturating the ghetto with lottery advertising that capitalizes on the desperate dream of escaping graffiti-strewn surroundings. Lottery officials are undeterred by the reality that poor people waste disproportionate dollars per capita on the vain hope of hitting the jackpot, thus at best diverting money needed for life's necessities and at worst ruining their lives with yet another addiction. How cynical can they get? And consider those big-name corporations splashing ads and logos across urban billboards, targeting potential consumers with sportswear so expensive that many can only procure it through funds from hold-ups, break-ins, and drug deals. Should a kid who can't afford a decent lunch spend $125 on basketball shoes?

Then there are sports executives who commercialize the misplaced ambitions of young Black men seeking recognition and fulfillment in sports rather in the professional workplace. True, sports has provided a level playing field for Blacks to compete with others in society, but even this has fostered false hopes that one can dribble and dunk his way to Easy Street. Every extra million contracted with pro basketball's Shaquille O'Neal and other star athletes only sparks the impossible dreams of inner city kids who wind up washing cars throughout their adult lives when they could have been learning to program computers, teach classes, perform surgeries–and in doing so support a family. But instead their talents are squandered, their lives a shadow of what they might have been.

One generation after the civil rights revolution with its all its hard-won protections and provisions, how has quality of life improved for African-American young people? Given the inroads of crime, drugs, illegitimate pregnancies and AIDS, are they possibly even worse off than before the social advances of the '60s?

## WOMEN IN THE BOARDROOM

The drive for racial equity in the '60s carried over into gender equality advances in the '70s. What fair-minded man could argue with equal pay for equal work, or defend the good-old-boy's glass ceiling that prevents the promotion of anyone wearing a skirt, no matter how skilled? While lamenting excesses of radical feminists with their unshaven armpits, we can celebrate their genuine successes. The liberation of women has enriched the lives of men as well. Everyone benefits when women are free to fulfil their God-given talents.

But has there been a downside to the women's liberation movement? After two decades, how much has society gained? "You've come a long way, baby!" boasts the Virginia Slims tobacco campaign. And how! Women are gaining equality with men in suffering lung cancer. What about the business world? While many have achieved satisfaction in boardrooms and professions, others acknowledge frustration, yearning to exchange their attache cases for an apron and come home to the kitchen. They want to raise their children themselves.

Such women with domestic ambitions are targets of ridicule from radical sisters. So what's all this rhetoric about feminist freedom? Can't all women decide for themselves whether to be attorneys or editors or housewives and mothers?

The liberation movement does promote a women's choice whether to have sex outside marriage. With what result? Check with TV heroine Murphy Brown. In 1992, it became a national joke when presidential candidate Dan Quayle suggested that she wasn't wise to pursue single parenthood. It's one thing to be forced into that situation by a man's abuse, adultery, or irresponsibility, but to otherwise choose to raise a child alone is no good–for mother or baby. No good for society, either.

It takes more than a village to raise a baby. It takes a dad, too.

Well, Quayle had no credibility with the Hollywood crowd and their millions of constituents. Hey, this is the guy who couldn't even spell "potato." But whatever his inadequacies in communicating about vegetables, the man was speaking wisdom here about people. Even Candace Bergen, the Murphy Brown actress, has belatedly acknowledged that perhaps Quayle was right after all–kids do need dads.

Mothers whose sons rob the neighborhood 7-Eleven often lament in self-recrimination: Where have I gone wrong? But even the best that the finest mother offers cannot atone for the lack of a functional father. Girls without a dad's affection tend toward promiscuity. Boys derive male identity from their fathers. Unless an uncle or trusted big brother figure fills the void, that boy may join a gang, which becomes a deadly substitute for paternal relationship. Gang membership combined with media violence in music, movies and video games is a deadly formula for producing criminals. But the same entertainment executives who ridiculed Dan Quayle insist that their products have no such influence on child consumers. (Why bite the hand that feeds you?) They blame firearms, mostly. Get rid of guns, and kids will be nice again.

Certainly, society must keep guns away from kids and criminals. But what about gun control in media programming? After the Columbine High School massacre, entertainment executives began to squirm under the scrutiny of accountability. Accomplishing real reform may require major boycotting of advertised products. Society should do whatever it takes to safeguard our young people so mothers can have better success shaping the character of their children.

## WOMEN IN THE BEDROOM

So much for motherhood. Now, what about the sexuality that turns a woman into a parent? Three decades into the sexual revolution, are women having a better time with sex and its aftermath?

One of society's obsessions is to copulate without consequences. This notion has caused untold trauma, to women especially. A woman typically invests her heart as well as her body into a sexual experience. She often bonds emotionally to her partner. Whereas sex can be an intensely emotional experience for men as well, Good-time Charlie can exit a relationship in search of new conquests without looking back. He's been a total jerk, but his woman somehow misses him. Years later she still may suffer a broken heart.

Evidently condoms can't prevent harm from illegitimate sex. They can't stretch around the heart to protect it from being ruptured. Condoms can't even guarantee prevention of venereal disease or pregnancies, due to their frequent failure from defects and misuse. So even assuming that passionate partners will be responsible enough to have brought "protection"–and be willing to accept this minimal restriction upon sexual expression–condoms are no cure-all, physically or emotionally.

When society spurns self-discipline and abstinence outside marriage, women end up the biggest losers. Men don't get pregnant. They may escape scot-free from parental responsibilities without ever realizing that they have engineered the conception of a human being. Some virile young studs have fathered half a dozen kids–that they know of–with no concern about paternal obligations. So the next twenty years and beyond, abandoned mothers must struggle alone with all the financial, emotional, and spiritual stresses of parenthood.

## ABORTION–A LIFESTYLE

Well aware of sexual inequity, many call for "reproductive freedom," by which they mean the liberty to terminate the unborn. But just think about what abortion has become in our society–far more than the act of terminating pregnancy. Abortion is a lifestyle, the way millions of men and women deal with difficulty. Struggling at school? Drop out–abort your education. Problems at work? Quit–abort your job. Has holy wedlock become unhappy deadlock? Divorce–abort your vows. Is God not performing well enough answering prayer? Quit church and abort your relationship with Him.

Too often, abortion attempts to escape the consequences of personal choices. With freedom must come responsibility. Scripture warns: "Do not be deceived, God is not mocked; for whatever a man sows, that he will also reap. For he who sows to his flesh will of the flesh reap corruption" (Galatians 6:7-8). Who could deny that America has both sown to the flesh and reaped corruption, with two thirds of urban births now out of wedlock? Legalizing abortion was supposed to reduce both illegitimate births and child abuse, but both have skyrocketed in the decades since Roe v. Wade.

Some suggest that abortion itself is the ultimate child abuse. It's more than removing fetal mass. There is a heart beating and a brain functioning, which raises suspicions that human life is developing. One thing is beyond dispute: Abortion means that some girl will never have birthday parties with friends, go shopping at the mall, or grow up to marry the man of her dreams. Some boy will never hit a baseball, polish up his car to go out on a date, or tell Bible stories to his grandchildren. Such is the high cost of somebody else's "reproductive freedom."

Abortive mothers often suffer their own sense of personal loss. For months and even years they may experience grief and guilt, particularly if their motive was escaping an inconvenient pregnancy. Why? One reason may be that mothers and babies bond while the baby is still in the womb. Medical science has shown that the unborn child learns to recognize mother's voice and is soothed by its sound.

Meanwhile, she is adjusting to her baby, both physically and emotionally. Not surprisingly, when a woman severs this bond, she often suffers assorted psycho-spiritual maladies. Moreover, if later in life she does wish to become a mother, she may be physically incapable of carrying a child to full term because of a previous abortion.

Secular feminists deny or downplay the danger and potential damage to a woman's own body, mind and soul in terminating the miracle of creation of a life from God. Such is the cruel gift of the gospel of personal preferences.

When it comes to guilt, the only true solution is the gospel of Jesus Christ. Rather than deny that a death happened in the womb, God calls us to accept the fact that another death took place at the cross. And when Jesus died, He assumed the guilt for sin of all kinds—even the guilt of Good-time Charlie and those who financially profit from an abortive woman's crisis. The Bible says: "All we like sheep have gone astray; we have turned, every one, to his own way; and the Lord has laid on Him the iniquity of us all" (Isaiah 53:6). Receiving Jesus is the only way to have peace with God and peace with ourselves. "If we say that we have no sin, we deceive ourselves, and the truth is not in us. If we confess our sins, He is faithful and just to forgive us our sins and to cleanse us from all unrighteousness" (1 John 1:8-9).

Whatever our feelings and convictions on this difficult and divisive subject, we might agree that abortion itself isn't the fundamental problem; it's an attempted solution to an untimely pregnancy. Most of the time, men initiate unwise or illicit sexual encounters, so they are primarily culpable when a desperate and abandoned woman gets an abortion. But don't expect paternal playboys to care much. The sexual liberation of women has provided men an abundance of playmates without holding them responsible for fatherhood. Society still glamorizes the bachelor who manipulates one liberated woman against the next. So why should he trade his sleek sports car for a minivan with child seats and diaper bags?

Finally recognizing that a good marriage provides shelter from the follies of unbridled singleness, some long-time feminists see new value in that traditional institution. Maybe it is nice after all to have a man around willing to share a lifelong covenant of fidelity. So those who watch Atlanta Braves baseball often see that icon of female independence, Jane Fonda, fondly clinging to Ted Turner's arm. He's her husband! She adores him so much she gave up her own public career for a lifestyle suspiciously similar to that of an old-fashioned housewife.

Whatever the mistakes and excesses of the women's liberation movement, notable accomplishments remain. Nothing has been more important than the protection of women against sexual harassment in the workplace. Equally vital has been outlawing the despicable tactic of casting blame upon the victim and questioning her integrity. Tragically, both of these invaluable gains for women were diminished during the recent scandals.

Back in the '60s, America sowed seeds of corruption, so today we have reaped a society experiencing moral chaos from our national leadership on down to our students—and their teachers. Campus activists have once again assaulted the schools with their radical agenda, only this time with their names engraved on the doors and desks of authority. Yesterday's anti-establishment protestors have become the backbone of the educational establishment. They also control much of our media and many local libraries. To a large extent, they run our government, from the local level on up. Their gospel of secular humanism has done much to deteriorate society.

"'Are they ashamed of their loathsome conduct? No, they have no shame at all; they do not even know how to blush. So they will fall among the fallen; they will be brought down when I punish them,' says the Lord" (Jeremiah 6:15 / NIV).

## ASSAULT ON CHRISTIANITY

America has nothing against the concept of a loving God. We need Him to fund our excesses and enable our dysfunctions. We want this God to be our friend, but not really our Father in heaven. We prefer a semi-senile grandfather up there who doesn't much care what we run around doing down here.

Angels? Sure! They watch over us as we go our own way and make sure nothing bad happens to us. And the moment we die they will escort us to heaven, where we can join in the big party up there.

Jesus? Cool. He's the best guru the world has ever seen. And wasn't He nice to everybody, telling us not to cast stones at each other or be judgmental? Just don't tell us He's the unique Son of God. And please, spare us from hearing about Christ's blood shed on the cross for our sins. That's ugly and unsophisticated, totally unsuited to the enlightened new millennium. Besides, just the notion of sin threatens our self-worth. We're just victims in need of emotional healing. At worst, we suffer some addictions. So what?

Such is the current thinking about religion. God's Ten Commandments are regarded as mere recommendations unable to discipline our transitory thoughts and ideas. So live by your own stars. Follow your feelings; do whatever makes you comfortable. Otherwise you risk becoming bigoted and narrow-minded.

Church? A great place to make business contacts and display public piety. Just give us a feel-good sermon about a God who provides strength to survive adversity and see our dreams fulfilled. No wonder that politicians in America have always loved churches. Where else on a Sunday morning can they find so many voters in one place, eager to be flattered and stroked?

In today's society, the only remaining sin seems to be intolerance. That is, unless you want to be intolerant of evangelical Christianity. Hollywood, while proclaiming diversity, tends to mock fervent believers who take Jesus and His claims seriously. But don't make fun of Eastern religions. Hollywood showcases the plight of Buddhists in Tibet while ignoring the millions of Christians oppressed and imprisoned by the same Chinese government.

In Sudan, thousands of believers are enslaved or raped, but don't expect any outcry from Western media or governments. After all, most Sudanese believers have dark skin, so they don't matter as much to us as if they had fair complexions like the Kosovo refugees. Besides, Chinese Christians in prison camps manufacture cheap goods that offer maximum value for our trade dollars. So just keep doing business with whoever can help us maintain our comfortable lifestyle, and we'll turn a deaf ear to the cries and moans of persecuted brothers and sisters.

How sad! In this past century more Christians have suffered and died for their faith than in either of the last two millennia–surpassing even the medieval persecutions. Does this matter to Western believers, at ease and secure in prosperous democratic societies?

Well, God cares.

## WEIGHED AND WANTING

Long ago the Lord predicted our age of greed and excess: "You have heaped up treasure in the last days" (James 5:3). He foresaw us chasing after the Dow on its run through the 11,000 mark. And so, He says, "You have lived on the earth in pleasure and luxury" (verse 5).

Is it wrong to live comfortably? Not unless we cross the line where comfort overcomes conviction and compassion, and profit is more valued than piety and propriety. Such a lifestyle will backfire on those who are "lovers of pleasure rather than lovers of God" (2 Timothy 3:4). And the resulting economic meltdown will burst upon us with terrifying suddenness.

"Come now, you rich, weep and howl for your miseries that are coming upon you! Your riches are corrupted, and your garments are moth-eaten. Your gold and silver are corroded, and their corrosion will be a witness against you and will eat your flesh like fire. Indeed the wages of the laborers who mowed your fields, which you kept back by fraud, cry out; and the cries of the reapers have reached the ears of the Lord" (James 5:1-5).

Tough words. God really cares about prison camp factories, illegal sweatshops, and slave farms where laborers are cheated out of their just compensation and benefits. It matters to Him when we formulate corporate policy and international relations based upon profit, thus making trading partners out of robber barons and oppressor nations.

So, yes, it's not "the economy, stupid!" Compassion counts more.

God warns: "You have fattened your hearts as in a day of slaughter" (verse 5).

Day of slaughter? Riots in our cities, perhaps? Food and fuel shortages? Maybe even bioterrorism? One little crop dusting plane dispersing several bags of anthrax bacteria could release a fatal payload over Washington, D.C. Millions might die. Poisoning the water supply for New York City would be frighteningly simple and surely would bring about a day of slaughter.

Some suggest the doom foretold in James 5 is associated with Y2K, the infamous computer glitch destined to strike at the stroke of midnight of the year 2000. Since you may be reading this book past that date, there's no need to venture a prediction about the severity of this digital nightmare. Depending on where in the world you live, you experienced something between the extremes of a minor disruption and TEOTWAWKI–The End Of The World As We Knew It. At minimum, Y2K is robbing the momentum from America's economic heyday, and doing even more damage overseas. In Western nations, probably the most immediate and universal effect of Y2K has been the panic of people who postponed preparations until the last minute, stampeding into supermarkets and banks.

It's amazing how much of economics in Western society runs on raw emotion. During the stock market boom of the glory days before Y2K, U.S. Fed chairman Allan Greenspan warned about "irrational exuberance"–exactly the type of mindset that eventually flips the opposite way and plunges society into panic. Even before Y2K, America was due for economic turmoil, having enjoyed unprecedented prosperity while 60 percent of the world's population was in severe recession or even depression. Economists long warned that one nation cannot thrive forever as an island of peak prosperity amid a sea of difficulty.

So to one extent or another, economic trouble is upon us. And all of it is fulfilling prophecy.

How tragically fitting that the incredible economic boom of the '90s was driven by computer technology. Computers became instruments of lust and greed, making the Internet a playground of sodomy and crass commercialism. Indeed, we "heaped together treasure for the last days." Every hoarded dollar bill boasts the lie: "In God We Trust." And consider the meaning of the year 2000. Two thousand years since what? The first appearance of Jesus Christ, as commonly understood. So this ought to be a celebration of Him. Instead we merrily prepared a party to end all parties, boasting of our successes and indulging our excesses. How appropriate then that with the stroke of the year 2000, the party would be over.

There is some historical precedent. Long ago there was a huge party in Babylon, the richest and most powerful nation in the world.

As the night wore on, drunken celebrants were so obsessed with merrymaking that they didn't realize a line had been crossed. Probation for their nation had ended. Suddenly a huge, bloodless finger burned these words into the palace wall: "Mene, mene, tekel upharsin," which translated means: "God has numbered your kingdom, and finished it. You have been weighed in the balances, and found wanting" (see Daniel 5:25-28).

"Weighed and wanting."

Fearful words. Do they apply to our own millennial situation?

When God says the party is over, it's not that He doesn't love us anymore. Indeed, He loves us all too much to enable our sinful dysfunctions and let us go on destroying ourselves and one another without some kind of divine intervention. Some are waking up in time to repent. For others, it will be forever too late.

## FEAR GOD!

For our planet in rebellion, God put a special message in the book of Revelation. It's particularly targeted for these last days, immediately before the return of Jesus Christ. So important is this message that it is symbolized by an angel of warning flying overhead. There is good news and bad news:

"Then I saw another angel flying in the midst of heaven, having the everlasting gospel to preach to those who dwell on the earth—to every nation, tribe, tongue, and people—saying with a loud voice, 'Fear God and give glory to Him, for the hour of His judgment has come; and worship Him who made heaven and earth, the sea and springs of water'" (Revelation 14:7,8).

The bad news for the world is that there is a judgment proceeding in heaven to which they are accountable. Like Babylon of old, they will be weighed and wanting unless they repent. Indeed, immediately following comes another angelic warning: "Babylon is fallen, is fallen, that great city, because she has made all nations drink of the wine of the wrath of her fornication" (Revelation 14:8). Obviously this isn't referring to literal Babylon, still in ruins. It's a warning for the last day coalition of organized evil and opposition to God. Later in these pages we will explore the full meaning of Babylon and its relevance to us today.

So the party will be over and God is holding the world accountable. This could be bad news, depending upon one's attitude and preparedness.

The good news is that there is still time to repent–turn around–and accept the everlasting gospel! This is God's message of salvation in Jesus Christ. The door is still open. The invitation for all who thirst for God's grace is: "Come ... whoever desires, let him take the water of life freely" (Revelation 22:17).

"Fear God, the everlasting Creator of heaven and earth!" the angel cries. Respect Him and stand in awe before the Judge of all the earth.

"Fear God, Hollywood! Forsake your celluloid sodomy and promote true values."

"Fear God, Wall Street! Forsake blind greed and show justice and mercy."

"Fear God, Washington! Forget opinion polls. Stand for the right though the heavens fall."

"Fear God, Silicone Valley! Employ technology as a blessing instead of a curse."

"Fear God, men who abuse women! Treat My daughters with dignity and love."

"Fear God, radical feminists! Respect my gift of creation life in the womb."

"Fear God, superficial religionists!" "Fear God and keep His commandments: for this is the whole duty of man" (Ecclesiastes 12:13 / KJV). Obey without attempting to achieve personal merit. Rather, true obedience is fueled by gratitude for God's free gift of Jesus Christ. "For this is the love of God, that we keep His commandments. And His commandments are not burdensome" (1 John 5:3).

"But wait," someone protests. "I thought we weren't supposed to fear God." Indeed, we need not be frightened of Him–if we find our fulfillment in Jesus Christ rather than in foolish counterfeits. Trusting in Jesus alone, we are safe. We need fear nothing about earth's final crisis, not Y2K, not an atomic attack or bioterrorism–nothing! For the sincere believer, "in the fear of the Lord there is strong confidence, and His children will have a place of refuge" (Proverbs 14:26).

A place of refuge! Lord, "You are my hiding place; You shall preserve me from trouble; You shall surround me with songs of deliverance" (Psalm 32:7). As most of the world hides from God on earth's last day, we can hide in God. Jesus will be "as a hiding place from the wind, and a cover from the tempest, as rivers of water in a dry place, as the shadow of a great rock in a weary land" (Isaiah 32:2).

Do you want Jesus to be your shelter amid all the millennimania threatening this world? You can arrange that with the Lord right now. If you are not sure how, please keep reading.

# 2 Chapter two
## DOME OF DOOM?

Ground zero for Millennimania is Jerusalem. Prophetic speculation swirls around that city. Supermarket tabloids go wild wondering what might happen there during the year 2000. Will Jesus descend in a UFO?

Many who trust the Bible over the tabloids also focus on Jerusalem. Some believe prophecy calls for a rebuilt Jewish temple there, run by priests who restore ancient animal sacrifices. They expect a seven-year tribulation during which the antichrist makes and then breaks a covenant with Jews. In their view Jesus will appear on the Mount of Olives and triumphantly enter the east gate to the new temple. In this view of final events, Christ will secretly rapture true believers–suddenly, invisibly, snatch them from the earth–before the tribulation, and afterward return with them to rule the world from Jerusalem.

The anticipated new worship center would be built on Jerusalem's Temple Mount. For two millennia, this speck of real estate has seen the fiercest turf wars in the history of the world! Jews, Muslims, and millions of Christians consider it sacred, particularly the site of the golden Dome of the Rock.

Will the Temple Mount be the launching pad for something wonderful like world peace at the return of Jesus? Or something terrible like World War III?

Perhaps both events? Or maybe neither?

Let's see what the Bible actually teaches. First, some further background.

The Dome of the Rock is a magnificent Muslim mosque. Jews, however, covet its location as supremely sacred because their ancestors worshiped there in a sanctuary King Solomon built. Then, 600 years before Christ was born in nearby Bethlehem, the Babylonian army destroyed Jerusalem's first temple. Another temple replaced it, only to suffer destruction by the Roman army in the year A.D. 70. With that temple destroyed and Jerusalem in ruins, Jewish people scattered across the Roman empire. Muslims eventually conquered Jerusalem with its Temple Mount and built their Dome over the ruins of the ancient Jewish sanctuary.

During succeeding centuries, various popes commissioned Crusades to win back Jerusalem. Armies of the Holy Roman Empire gained and then lost possession of the city. As the 20th century dawned, Muslim Palestinians controlled the Holy Land, with a few Jewish settlers trickling in. More Jews immigrated after World War I. Following World War II, refugees from the European Holocaust returned to their ancient homeland, where they established a nation in 1948. Then during the dramatic Six-Day War of 1967 the Israelis recaptured Jerusalem.

Many Jews believe God gave Jerusalem back to them in preparation for building a third temple. They join millions of Christians in believing that a rebuilt temple would fulfil the prophetic blueprint.

There's just one obstacle—a huge one. The Temple Mount remains occupied by Muslims. In fact, the Dome of the Rock is one of Islam's holiest shrines. Arabs everywhere would eagerly die to prevent Jews from building a temple there.

So what will happen? Does the Dome doom world peace?

## PREPARING FOR A NEW TEMPLE

Most Israelis, both secular and religious, don't want to wage war on the Temple Mount. Even many who yearn to see the temple rebuilt are content to let the soon-expected messiah do it. Some, though, are diligently preparing behind the scenes to build the new temple themselves. Architectural plans exist; rumors have it that stones are being cut.

Rebuilding the temple itself would not be enough to restore services. Numerous intricate ornaments, utensils, bowls and altars are needed. Since 1978, a group known as the Temple Institute has constructed most of the tools needed for use in temple service—garments for the priests, musical instruments, vessels for carrying blood, a brazen laver, and so on.

What about priests to administer the new temple? According to an Associated Press report, a Jerusalem-based religious group, the "Movement for Establishing the Temple," has been recruiting ultra-Orthodox parents to dedicate their boys to the Jewish priestly caste known as "Cohenim."

Let's pause and summarize. Preparations already well underway for the temple itself, its utensils, and even priests in training. What about sacrificial animals? Recently there was a flurry of excitement over the discovery of a red heifer named Melody, originally believed to be the first of its kind born in the Holy Land in two millennia. But later, white hairs were spotted on the young cow's tail and she was deemed impure.

Melody's disqualification brought a sigh of relief to many in Israel. One legislator had warned: "'That cow represents the risk of a massive religious war.' said Avraham Poraz, a member of the parliament from the leftist Meretz Party. 'If the fanatics get ahold of it and try to take over the Temple Mount, God knows what will happen.'"

Indeed, only God knows what the zealots will risk in rebuilding the temple. They are confident that soon they will have their red heifer. Millions of Christians are praying that they do.

Does Bible prophecy endorse all this excitement about a rebuilt temple in Jerusalem with a renewed priesthood—complete with animal sacrifices? Let's look at seven challenges to this scenario.

## 1) JESUS THE ONLY SACRIFICE FOR SIN

What really disqualified Melody the cow from serving as a valid sacrifice for sin was not a few white hairs on her tail. On the cross two thousand years ago, Jesus Christ became the full and final sacrifice for sin: "Behold! The Lamb of God who takes away the sin of the world!" (John 1:29). So all this enthusiasm about a red heifer amounts to nothing but "dead works" (Hebrews 9:14). Despite their fervent hopes and prayers, those who imagine that further animal sacrifices in a new temple are needed to fulfil God's purposes have fallen prey to false religion. Blasphemy, in fact.

## 2) JESUS THE ONLY HIGH PRIEST

With two thousand years having passed since Christ's sacrifice for our sin, how do we connect with its benefits today? The Bible says: "We have an Advocate with the Father, Jesus Christ the Righteous" (1 John 2:1). "For there is one God and one Mediator between God and men, the Man Christ Jesus," (1 Timothy 2:5). "It is Christ who died, and furthermore is also risen, who is even at the right hand of God, who also makes intercession for us" (Romans 8:34).

So Jesus is our advocate, mediator, and intercessor. All these job titles point to His work as our High Priest, begun after His resurrection and ascension to heaven's throne: "Seeing then that we have a great High Priest who has passed through the heavens, Jesus the Son of God, let us hold fast our confession. For we do not have a High Priest who cannot sympathize with our weaknesses, but was in all points tempted as we are, yet without sin. Let us therefore come boldly to the throne of grace, that we may obtain mercy and find grace to help in time of need" (Hebrews 4:14-16).

When overwhelmed by guilt, fear, weakness, or confusion, how wonderful to come with confidence to God through Jesus, our High Priest. No enemy has the right to blame us or shame us. Jesus stands up for us against all attacks and accusations.

The Bible says: "He has a permanent priesthood" (Hebrews 7:24 / NIV). That means there is no place in God's plan for anyone else in that role, now and forever. So anyone claiming to be another high priest in Jerusalem would be a competitor, a counterfeit to Christ. And didn't Jesus Himself warn again such imposters in the last days? (see Matthew 24:24).

## 3) JESUS BUILDS THE NEW TEMPLE

Just as a cook needs a kitchen, our High Priest needs a temple in which to serve. Since Jesus is now in heaven, that's where we might expect to find His temple. Sure enough, the Bible says: "Christ has not entered the holy places made with hands, ... but into heaven itself, now to appear in the presence of God for us" (Hebrews 9:24).

You may recall Christ's words declaring the Jewish temple null and void. He warned the priests and leaders there: "See! Your house is left to you desolate" (Matthew 23:38). When Jesus died several days later, God tore apart the sacred veil of Jerusalem's temple, signifying the end of legitimate worship there. Ultimately, this temple was burned in the Roman invasion. Josephus, the historian, noted that soldiers digging for gold that had melted into the cracks between the foundation stones overturned them, just as Jesus had predicted (see Matthew 24:1,2).

"Now this is the main point of the things we are saying: We have such a High Priest, who is seated at the right hand of the throne of the Majesty in the heavens, a Minister of the sanctuary and of the true tabernacle which the Lord erected, and not man" (Hebrews 8:1-2). So any temple on earth built by human hands would then be a false tabernacle, an unauthorized imitation.

## 4) JESUS POINTS TO THE NEW JERUSALEM

Jerusalem has the richest history and heritage of any city in the world. When London, Paris and Washington, D.C., were still grassy fields, Jerusalem was the center of God's salvation activity. This changed after Jesus died on the cross and rose from the dead to heaven's New Jerusalem. And so the New Testament calls away from "the present city of Jerusalem, because she is in slavery with her children. But the Jerusalem that is above is free, and she is our mother" (Galatians 4:25-26 / NIV).

Rather than calling us back to old Jerusalem, the Bible says: "You have come to ... the heavenly Jerusalem, ... to Jesus the Mediator of the new covenant" (Hebrews 12:22-24). According to the book of Revelation, this New Jerusalem will eventually descend from heaven to this earth, like a giant space city: "Now I saw a new heaven and a new earth, for the first heaven and the first earth had passed away. Also there was no more sea. Then I, John, saw the holy city, New Jerusalem, coming down out of heaven from God, prepared as a bride adorned for her husband. And I heard a loud voice from heaven saying, 'Behold, the tabernacle of God is with men, and He will dwell with them, and they shall be His people. God Himself will be with them and be their God'" (Revelation 21:1-3).

When will this happen? Notice the context: the immediate aftermath of Revelation 20, which speaks of the one thousand years we will spend in heaven with Jesus after He comes. So only after another millennium has passed with us in heaven will the New Jerusalem descend with Jesus and His people and settle upon this earth made new.

Meanwhile, nothing can be clearer than this: true prophecy points to Jesus in the heavenly temple of the New Jerusalem, while false prophecy anticipates fulfillment in a counterfeit temple built by human hands in old Jerusalem.

## 5) JESUS FULFILS THE COVENANT

A most exciting spiritual phenomenon these days is the increasing number of Jews accepting Jesus. Many are won by mathematical proof that He is their Messiah, or Savior/King. One half millennium before Jesus was born, Daniel communicated this prediction in exquisite detail.

Daniel chapter 9 begins with the aged prophet in deep distress because God seems not to be fulfilling His covenant with the Jewish nation (see verse 4). Frightened that their sins might be causing this, Daniel offers one of the most heartfelt prayers of all Scripture, summing up: "O Lord, hear! O Lord, forgive! O Lord, listen and act! Do not delay" (verse 19).

Deeply touched, God sends the angel Gabriel to assure Daniel that Messiah would appear as promised, after all. He then specifies: "Seventy weeks are determined for your people and for your holy city, to finish the transgression, to make an end of sins, to make reconciliation for iniquity, to bring in everlasting righteousness" (verse 24). In other words, God was giving the Jews a probationary time of 70 weeks to stop trifling with transgression and prepare for their sin-conquering Messiah.

When would this calendar countdown get started?: "From the going forth of the command to restore and build Jerusalem until Messiah the Prince, there shall be seven weeks and sixty-two weeks" (verse 25).

Let's decode this intriguing prophecy–a time span of 7 weeks plus 62 weeks–totaling 69 weeks. The starting point was a special command to rehabilitate Jerusalem, destroyed during the Babylonian invasion. These 69 weeks would then stretch from the time of that command until Messiah's appearance.

Fascinated so far? Let's proceed with some quick calculations. Sixty-nine weeks equals a year and a third–specifically 483 days. Strange, you may say, it was actually more like almost 500 years from when Jerusalem was rebuilt until the time of Jesus. And that is correct–483 years, to be precise. You see, the word translated "weeks" literally means "sevens." And this could be a unit of seven days or a unit of seven years. Watching Daniel 9 in action, it's evident that God gave a time prophecy with 69 units of seven years each, totaling 483 years.

Do you see it? This prophecy foretold that 483 years would separate the time of the command to rebuild Jerusalem and the time Messiah would appear. Let's investigate whether that really happened.

First we must discover the time when the decree went forth empowering Jewish exiles to restore the city of Jerusalem. No need to guess about that date. The Old Testament records this decree in the seventh year of the Persian king Artaxerxes, which was 457 B.C. (see Ezra 7:11-13). This date has been confirmed by modern discoveries in archeology, a fact recognized by many Bible scholars. The widely-acclaimed Encyclopedia of Bible Difficulties, for example, endorses the year 457 B.C. as the fulfillment of Daniel 9. This book by Zondervan, a familiar evangelical publisher, explains how the prophecy unfolds:

"If, then, the decree of 457 granted to Ezra himself is taken as the ... commencement of the ... 483 years, we come out to the precise year of the appearance of Jesus of Nazareth as Messiah (or Christ): 483 minus 457 comes out to A.D. 26. But since a year is gained in passing from 1 B.C. to A.D. 1 (there being no such year as zero), it actually comes out to A.D. 27–a most remarkable exactitude in the fulfillment of such an ancient prophecy."[1]

So there it is, mathematical proof that Jesus is the Messiah. In A.D. 27—the same year foretold by Daniel 9–Jesus became anointed in that role at His baptism. He went forth announcing that the "time is fulfilled" (Mark 1:15).

What time was He talking about? The prophetic time of Daniel 9–the 69 weeks of years that would introduce "Messiah the Prince." A prophetic fulfillment of amazing precision! You can see a diagram of all this in the chart below.

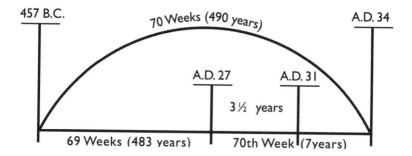

And there's more. You may recall that when Jesus began His miracles, the religious leaders tried continually to put Him to death. But again and again Christ escaped. The gospel of John records one such episode:

"Then they sought to take Him; but no one laid a hand on Him, because His hour had not yet come" (John 7:30).

Was there a specific date set apart for Jesus to die? Everyone knows His public ministry lasted three-and-a-half years. This time period also was foretold in Bible prophecy as a calendar countdown to Calvary. The evening before Jesus died, He prayed, "Father, the hour has come" (John 17:1). It was the time foretold by Daniel 9–precisely in the middle of an additional week of years beyond the original 69 weeks ending with His baptism. Notice: "In the middle of the week He shall bring an end to sacrifice and offering" (Daniel 9:27).

The middle of that 70th week of seven years, of course, would be three and a half years after Jesus began his ministry. And that's exactly when He ended the age of sacrifices and sin offerings by His death. That's when the veil of the temple was torn in two, ending the significance of Jewish temple services.

So Jesus confirmed the covenant God had made with His people by coming right on schedule and dying as Messiah. This brings us to the most perplexing part of the popular prophetic scenario. Somehow, believe it or not, many Christians take this convincing prophecy about Jesus and commit it to the antichrist. They actually remove Jesus from Daniel 9:27 and substitute the antichrist!

Without question, this covenant in Daniel 9 verses 4 and 27 refers to Christ's saving work. Besides, nothing anywhere in Scripture teaches that the antichrist will either make or break any kind of covenant with anybody. Actually, if the antichrist attacked a rebuilt temple in Jerusalem and ended its blasphemous animal sacrifices, it would be a blessing of desolation, not the "abomination" of desolation (Daniel 9:27). That's something worth careful consideration.

Remember that, of all the prophecies which confirm Jesus as Messiah, Daniel 9 is one of the most persuasive and powerful. Thousands of Jewish people have concluded that Jesus is indeed Messiah because of its mathematical evidence.

## 6) JESUS HEADS A NEW ISRAEL

Now we are prepared to consider the prophetic significance of Israel. Are Jewish people the exclusive inheritors of God's covenant with Abraham?

Interestingly, Muslims consider themselves the true children of Abraham ("Ibrahim," they say) because Ishmael their forefather was his firstborn son. But Ishmael was conceived outside the covenant of faith which God had established with Abraham. This immediately disqualifies Muslims from being the covenant people of God.

Muslims consider the Koran their holy book. It promotes high moral principles but does not teach that Jesus died as our Savior and rose from the dead to be our Lord. Thus Islam lacks the faith principle necessary to come under God's covenant.

The Bible is clear: "Know that only those who are of faith are sons of Abraham" (Galatians 3:7). So the only hope for Muslims to become true children of Abraham is by reflecting his faith in the Messiah of the covenant.

Jewish people have descended from Isaac, Abraham's faith-child through whom God's covenant was to be fulfilled. But does this mean they can automatically claim Abraham as their spiritual father?

That question came up back in Christ's day. The religious leaders of the Jews felt no need of Jesus, claiming to be secure in God's favor already as children of Abraham. But Jesus responded, "If you were Abraham's children, you would do the works of Abraham" (John 8:39).

Remember, having the blood of Abraham is not enough to be children of Abraham. One must share the faith of Abraham in the Messiah of the covenant. Yet what did Israel do with its Messiah? Unfortunately, for the most part,"His own did not receive Him" (John 1:11). Leaders of the nation crucified Christ.

Still God's mercy lingered. Instead of immediately sending His disciples around the Roman empire with the gospel, the resurrected Christ sent them first to the lost sheep of the house of Israel, beginning with Jerusalem. This was because the Jewish nation still had left to them three-and-a-half years of national probation—the last half of the 70th week in Daniel 9. But time was short. Those 490 years of opportunity to accept the covenant would expire in A.D. 34.

What did Israel do with its final years of opportunity? Thousands of individual Jews accepted Jesus, but the nation itself sealed its rejection of the covenant. After stoning God's messenger Stephen (see Acts 7), they launched a great persecution against fellow Jews who believed in Jesus. At this point the apostles declared: "It was necessary that the word of God should be spoken to you first; but since you reject it, and judge yourselves unworthy of everlasting life, behold, we turn to the Gentiles" (Acts 13:46).

Jesus had warned Jewish leaders this would happen: "The kingdom of God will be taken from you and given to a nation bearing the fruits of it" (Matthew 21:43). So now the covenant promises were removed from the nation of Israel as a whole and given to believers in Jesus, both Jews and Gentiles: "If you are Christ's then you are Abraham's seed, and heirs according to the promise" (Galatians 3:29; see also Ephesians 2:13-19).

Many Jews today are indeed children of Abraham, not because of their flesh but through their faith in Jesus as Messiah. Multitudes more will accept him, according to Scripture. But Abraham's covenant now belongs not to one particular nation but to anyone who believes in Jesus.

Can non-Jews really be children of Abraham? In Christ, yes: "But you are a chosen generation, a royal priesthood, a holy nation, His own special people ... who once were not a people but are now the people of God" (1 Peter 2:9-10).

These days, the land God once gave His people is anything but holy. Former president Jimmy Carter recounts a trip to Israel in his book, The Blood of Abraham. He tells of visiting several kibbutzim, or Jewish settlements, near the Sea of Galilee. One Sabbath he dropped in on the local synagogue in a community of several hundred and was shocked to find only two other worshipers present.

Later, when the Carters visited Prime Minister Golda Meir, the conversation drifted into religion. Carter commented about the general lack of spiritual interest among the Israelis. The prime minister agreed but said she wasn't concerned because of the Orthodox Jews around. She added with a laugh, "If you attend a session of the Knesset [the Israeli parliament], you will see them in action and will know they have not lost their faith."[2]

Surely, Orthodox Jews today have not lost their zeal. But could we call it faith? Faith in the Messiah of the covenant? Remember: "Only those who are of faith are sons of Abraham" (Galatians 3:7). Enlightened Bible scholars know that the Old Testament is not primarily Israel-centered, but Messiah-centered. Everything depends upon accepting the Messiah.

These days there's a lot of excitement about political advances in the nation of Israel during the last half century. Nobody can deny that remarkable things have happened. But how can they qualify as a fulfillment of God's covenant to Abraham when Israel as a whole still rejects Jesus? Indeed, sharing the good news about Christ publicly is next to impossible throughout the nation. Even blood Jews who trust in Jesus as Messiah have not been welcome in Israel to the same immigration benefits as unbelievers.

Well, if the fulfillment of God's covenant to Abraham is not happening in Israel, what else is going on there? Recall that Jesus warned against false prophets in the last days with their false predictions concerning His coming. Could all the attention showered upon unbelieving Israel be a smoke screen of the enemy to divert sincere Christians from the real issues concerning Christ's coming, raising false prophetic expectations?

## 7) JESUS WILL RETURN IN GLORY

Christians everywhere are excited about the rapture. Their bumper stickers declare: "If I'm Raptured Take the Wheel." "Warning: Driver Will Be Raptured Any Moment."

It might be intriguing to vanish suddenly from the earth. But is this what the Bible teaches about Christ's second coming? Let's check it out.

First we find that the word "rapture" itself is not in the English Bible. It comes from a Latin word meaning "to carry away," to be carried away when the Lord comes. The word translated "rapture" shows up in the Latin version of 1 Thessalonians 4:16-17.

"For the Lord Himself will descend from heaven with a shout, with the voice of the archangel, and with the trumpet of God. And the dead in Christ will rise first. Then we who are alive and remain shall be caught up together [raptured] with them in the clouds to meet the Lord in the air. And thus we shall ever be with the Lord."

Picture the scene! Jesus coming from heaven, bursting through the clouds to rescue us, shouting for joy. Then a mighty blast from God's trumpet. This will be the most vocal, spectacular event of all time! Nothing secret about it whatsoever!

Anyway, why would Jesus want to sneak us up to heaven? He's waited two millennia to come and get His people. Why shouldn't it be a triumphant event? Everyone on earth, saved or lost, will know when Jesus returns to gather His elect saints. "Then the sign of the Son of Man will appear in heaven, and then all the tribes of the earth will mourn, and they will see the Son of Man coming on the clouds of heaven with power and great glory. And He will send His angels with a great sound of a trumpet, and they will gather together His elect" (Matthew 24:30-31).

The Bible does say Christ will come unexpectedly like a thief in the night. But does this mean the world won't realize when it's happening?

Consider Pearl Harbor on the fateful morning of December 7, 1941. Though American intelligence had warned of an imminent Japanese attack, it came as a surprise. But when those bombers dived out of the sky, everyone knew what was happening. So it will be at the return of Jesus. Despite worldwide warnings, the unsaved will be caught by surprise. But they certainly will be aware of Christ's presence.

What will happen to those unready to meet Jesus? Will they have further opportunity to repent, perhaps under less than ideal circumstances? Or will human probation end at the coming of Christ? Let's see what Jesus taught:

"And as it was in the days of Noah, so it will be also in the days of the Son of Man: They ate, they drank, they married wives, they were given in marriage, until the day that Noah entered the ark, and the flood came and destroyed them all" (Luke 17:26-27).

Total destruction, just as in the days of Noah. The world, then as now, was engrossed in business as usual until God's final, fatal surprise. All who neglected His warning lost their lives. "Even so shall it be in the day when the Son of Man is revealed" (verse 30).

After Christ's coming, bodies will be scattered across the earth. Those left behind are all dead: "'Two people will be in one bed; one will be taken and the other left. Two women will be grinding grain together; one will be taken and the other left.' 'Where, Lord?' they asked. He replied, 'Where there is a dead body, there the vultures will gather'" (Luke 17:36-37 / NIV).

Apparently the secret rapture isn't Scriptural. It's rooted in a medieval myth recently popularized among Protestants, as we will see in the pages ahead.

No, Jesus will not need to sneak His people away from this earth and up to heaven. His second coming will be the most magnificent and spectacular event in human history, and everyone will know it.

## NO DOOM IN THE DOME

Meanwhile, there is no doom for us at Jerusalem's Dome of the Rock. Turmoil may continue over there, but not the fulfilling of God's covenant. Beware of false prophecy and all other millennimania. Our hope is not in old Jerusalem but in the New Jerusalem, where Jesus intercedes for us in heaven's temple. Soon He will keep His promise: "I will come again and receive you to Myself; that where I am, there you may be also" (John 14:3).

Have you made arrangements to go with Him on that day? Just now you can confess yourself a sinner and claim Him as Savior. "Now is the day of salvation" (2 Corinthians 6:2).

---

[1] Gleason L. Archer, *Encyclopedia of Bible Difficulties*, (Grand Rapids, Mich.: Zondervan, 1982), p. 290.

[2] Jimmy Carter, *The Blood of Abraham*, (New York: Houghton Mifflin, 1985), pp. 8, 9.

# Chapter three
## TOXIC CHRISTIANITY

It happened on a nice spring morning at Columbine High School. Lunchtime began as usual, with the cafeteria serving its daily opportunity for bantering and bravado. Up in the library, pages rustled as students busied themselves with homework. This was a favorite time and place for Cassie Bernall to fortify her soul with Scripture. Meanwhile, fellow seniors Eric Harris and Dylan Klebold armed themselves with tragically different ammunition.

The carnage began in the parking lot, then moved indoors. After tossing bombs and spraying bullets around the cafeteria, the gunmen charged up the stairs toward the library. Hallways echoed with the deafening staccato of high-powered bullets mingled with screams of terror and pain. Inside the library, a frantic teacher called 911 and yelled for students to hit the floor. Cassie began quietly calling upon God

Then the killers burst in and began shooting. One of them saw Cassie praying and decided to challenge her faith. Pointing his rifle at her head, he demanded to know whether she really believed in God.

It was the climactic moment of that hellish day. Cassie knew that confessing her Lord would be pronouncing her own death sentence. What would her answer be?

"Yes!"

A bullet exploded into her temple. Cassie became a martyr for her faith.

The killers showcased the kingdom of Satan. They were the final product of a toxic culture that worships weaponry and gorges itself on a gruesome concoction of Marilyn Manson shock rock, movies such as Natural Born Killers, and violent video games.

Cassie represented the kingdom of God. She personified a virtuous and vibrant Christian environment that brings joy and fulfillment in worshiping, trusting and serving Jesus. God's grace had saved Cassie's soul out of darkness and transported her into the light of His love. She became sweet, happy, focused, and responsible.

Even the secular media could not ignore the contrast in character between Cassie and her killers. Good versus evil. Hope versus hate. Something worth dying for versus nothing worth living for.

## POISONED ZEAL

Besides the two competing cultures of toxic carnality and wholesome Christianity, a third category invites investigation: toxic Christianity, represented by another teenager, Simeon Stylites.

Simeon's religion was bleak and harsh, like the Syrian desert where he was a shepherd long ago in the early fifth century. Seeking peace with God, Simeon quit his flock and joined a monastery. Soon his intense spiritual quest drove him into total solitude. He fasted from food during the entire Lenten season, seeking to subdue the flesh so the Spirit could rule his life. To no avail. Still dissatisfied with his spiritual progress, Simeon disciplined himself to stand upright for long periods of time.

Let's pause to assess those teenage lives and what they represented. Simeon's character was obviously much different than the killers of Columbine. He pursued good rather than evil and sinlessness rather than satanism.

So did Cassie. She shared Simeon's wholehearted dedication to God, but this was about all they had in common. Whereas Cassie enjoyed an abundant life in Jesus, full of fruitful relationships, Simeon shunned all friendships. Rather than loving lost people for Jesus, Simeon avoided contact with them. Fearing the world's temptations, he withdrew from it instead of trying to make a difference for Christ. And so his life became barren and useless, lacking the spiritual satisfaction and fulfillment Cassie shared with everyone privileged to know her.

Simeon took his solitary strictures to such extremes that in the year 423 he mounted a nine foot pillar to escape the world. His pillars got taller and taller as he imagined himself getting closer and closer to God. He finally died atop a pillar 50 feet high, never having realized the perfection he so earnestly sought.

How sad. It's one thing to take a break from the world for a few days and get alone with God. Such relaxation is emotionally refreshing and spiritually recharging. But Simeon, seeking perfection before God, just got away and stayed away from people.

Another major difference between Cassie and Simeon: Whereas she found rest and fulfillment in Jesus, he saw Christ primarily as an example for sinlessness. Indeed, Christ is our example, but first and foremost He is our Savior. Jesus said: "Be of good cheer, I have overcome the world" (John 16:33). But rather than finding refuge in Christ's accomplishments, Simeon focused upon his own spiritual attainments. He compared himself with Jesus but sadly, and perhaps unconsciously, competed with Him instead of trusting in His life, death and resurrection to find acceptance with God.

The Bible teaches: "Pure and undefiled religion before God and the Father is this: to visit orphans and widows in their trouble, and to keep oneself unspotted from the world" (James 1:27). Simeon was right in seeking to remain unspotted from the world but wrong to seclude himself from helping widows and orphans. Thus he forfeited true religion and fell under the spell of toxic Christianity.

So it was that a dedicated teenager became the weird spectacle of a hermit imprisoned in his own small world of sanctified selfishness. Nevertheless, the Christian church venerated Simeon Stylites as a spiritual hero. Upon his death the cities of Antioch and Constantinople competed for the possession of his body. For six centuries ascetics known as pillar saints followed Simeon's example by living up on pillars away from the world, pursuing their own personal perfection.

## SAINT SALLY

How could it be that the church could emulate and even venerate such an imbalanced, dysfunctional religionist? Because Christianity itself had fallen prey to a toxic culture where misplaced zeal overpowered enlightened faith. Believers ready to sacrifice life itself rather than yield their commitment to Christ allowed their faith to be corrupted with legalistic pagan influences. They adopted false teachings which suffocated the gospel of God's grace. Quietly and gradually the apostasy spread. Although many believers refused to compromise gospel truth, the church in general suffered a serious loss of faith.

Should this surprise us? Had not God's people throughout history continually wandered from His will? The New Testament even predicted problems within the church. Peter the apostle warned, "There will be false teachers among you, who will secretly bring in destructive heresies. ... And many will follow their destructive ways" (2 Peter 2:1-2). Paul also prophesied that truth would suffer (see Acts 20:29-30).

All kinds of pagan rites and ceremonies which Christ and the apostles never heard of infiltrated Christianity. Around the third century, penance entered to prevent repenting sinners from rejoicing in sins forgiven and the assurance of complete acceptance with God. Then in the early fifth century, legalism ascended to new heights with Simeon Stylites.

Then there was Origen, a respected and eloquent defender of Christianity in its early centuries. He taught that "perfect" saints, or those nearly so, enjoyed special access to God. So-called "simple" believers, however, had to content themselves with lesser blessings. Those who seemed closest to perfection became objects of veneration. Their prayers were coveted as if they had a hotline to God through superior piety. Images in their honor sprouted all over.

All this is foreign to the gospel, which declares us all equal: equally lost without Jesus and equally saved if we believe in Him. The Bible says there is no difference among us in terms of personal merit (Romans 3:23). We are either saved or lost. There are no second-class Christians—and no super-saints who stand more acceptable before God than any believer, no matter how pathetic and embarrassing our struggles may be.

It helps to know the Bible definition of a saint. It's someone who has chosen to be "set apart for God," that is, living a God-centered life instead of a self-centered life. Sainthood does not depend upon how successful we are in overcoming bad habits. All who commit themselves to God, trusting in Jesus, qualify as saints in good and regular standing despite whatever failures may remain.

You've heard about Saint Paul, Saint John, Saint Matthew. Well, if you're a Christian, put your own name in there. Saint Sam. Saint Sally. Saint Bill. How about that!

Sainthood for struggling believers is such good news it's often hard to get hold of. When we accept Jesus as our Savior, God can suddenly and completely consider us as perfect as He is. And all believers equally share Christ's perfect record of righteousness.

## BACK TO EDEN

Come with me far away to the garden of Eden. It's the end of creation week. Everything is beautiful and peaceful. Lush green meadows sparkle with wild flowers. Rivers race through fragrant forests and pour into waterfalls. Exotic birds of all colors frolic among the trees, their songs a harmony of praise. Then God creates a beautiful woman as His crowning masterpiece and presents her to Adam. He gives them together the custody of their paradise garden home.

As the sun is about to set on the sixth day of creation week, God looks around and nods approvingly. Everything is good, as perfect as He Himself can make it.

What happened next? "Then God blessed the seventh day and sanctified it, because in it He rested from all His work which God had created and made" (Genesis 2:3). This word sanctified is just like its cousin word saint, meaning "set apart for God." (Some Bible versions translate the word as "holy." Therefore "holy" and "sanctified" mean the same thing—that which is dedicated exclusively to God.)

So God set apart the seventh day for rest. Not that He was tired! No, He set aside the Sabbath for us to celebrate with Him His accomplishment in our creation. Adam and Eve had done nothing themselves to earn the right to rest, yet God invited them to share the joy of His creation.

You may know that Jesus is the Creator of the world (see John chapter 1 and Hebrews chapter 1). So the Sabbath has special meaning for Christians. In fact, Sabbath rest in Christ's finished work symbolizes what Christianity stands for. Other world religions focus upon self-improvement, what they can do to better themselves, but we Christians celebrate Christ's accomplishments on our behalf. That's why the Sabbath points us away from ourselves, away from our works, to trust in what Jesus has done for us.

The Sabbath also provides rich insight into the meaning of Calvary. Let's reverently go to the cross on that fatal Friday afternoon. How things have changed since that first Friday on creation week! In place of beautiful meadows and mountains we see the bare rocks of Golgotha, the place of the skull. Instead of the sweet songs of the birds of paradise, we hear the mocking shout: "Crucify Him!"

Yes, so much has changed. But one thing remains the same on this Friday afternoon. Once again Jesus is completing a work for humanity. With His dying breath He cries: "It is finished!" (John 19:30). Mission accomplished! A world redeemed!

Then, as the sun begins to set, friends of Jesus lay Him to rest inside a tomb. There He remains over Sabbath hours to memorialize His completed work for our salvation. After His quiet Sabbath repose Jesus arises and ascends to heaven's royal throne.

Do you see it? The Sabbath memorializes Christ's two greatest accomplishments— creating us and saving us. These are the reasons above all others why we worship Him. How appropriate then that we make the Sabbath our special day of worship.

In this age of atheism and evolutionism, the world has forgotten its Creator. And with all the confusion about self-sufficiency and self-realization, the world has forgotten its Savior. No wonder God says: "'Remember the Sabbath, to keep it holy' [Exodus 20:8]. Remember that I made you and I saved you. Set the Sabbath apart for Me, even as I have set it apart for you."

How much we need the Sabbath! So often in our busy lives we hurry through the week, out of time and out of touch with God and with each other. The Sabbath is God's invitation to take an entire day apart from life's responsibilities to enjoy with Him and with fellow believers. And beyond the benefits of rest and refreshment, we express faith in Him as our Maker and Redeemer by entering His Sabbath rest.

Let's probe deeper into the Sabbath as a symbol of salvation. God's Law demands that all our work be faithfully performed and finished: "Six days shalt thou labor and do all thy work" (Exodus 20:9 / KJV). This presents a problem, because when the sun goes down each Friday afternoon–even after a long week of working hard–we have to acknowledge lots of unfinished business. But God invites us to rest anyway–not because of our accomplishments but because of His! And so, right there among all the duties required by the Ten Commandments, God offers us rest from our unfinished works by reminding us of His perfect work on our behalf.

The devil knows that many who try to please God wind up trusting in their own works for salvation. No wonder Satan hates Sabbath rest. Week by week the Sabbath assures believers that despite our shortcomings, we stand complete in Christ. What tremendous therapy for legalism! Finally we have relief from those awful feelings about not being good enough. There's no need now to worry about penance or working our way back into God's favor. This is the beautiful message of the Sabbath!

As our Creator and Savior, Jesus proclaimed Himself "Lord of the Sabbath" (Matthew 12:8). He kept the Sabbath holy all His life, and He never taught that the day which memorializes His work should be changed over to Sunday. So how and when did that change happen?

## DAY OF SUN WORSHIP

Discovering the origins of Sunday keeping takes us on a fascinating tour of early Christian history. First century believers wanted to distance themselves from anything Jewish. The Jews, you see, had angered the emperor by constantly revolting to regain their national independence.

Rome struck back. In A.D. 70, Roman armies stormed Jerusalem. A quarter million Jews were starved, burned, crucified or otherwise killed. Numerous anti-Jewish riots swept the empire, climaxed by even stiffer penalties for Jews.

Because Christians and Jews shared the same heritage, Romans regarded both groups as basically the same. This was unfair. Christians wanted peace with the government, rendering to Caesar his due. But they suffered anyway, just as if they were Jews—beyond the persecution already theirs for Christ's sake.

After another Jewish rebellion, the Romans again destroyed Jerusalem in the year 135. Emperor Hadrian outlawed Jewish worship—notably their Sabbath keeping. Christians felt compelled to sever themselves totally from their Hebrew heritage. Gradually they welcomed customs and holy days from the pagan culture of the Roman empire, including the weekly day of sun worship.

For several centuries, Christians kept both the Sabbath and the day of the sun.. Slowly, the first day of the week gained more and more prominence. This side-by-side practice continued into the sixth century, with the true Sabbath still holding firm in many areas. But finally the Sunday eclipsed the Sabbath throughout the empire, although even then pockets of Sabbath keepers remained here and there.

The Epistle of Barnabas, written around the year 135, contains the first definite reference to keeping Sunday. It's interesting to notice the case presented there for abandoning the Sabbath.

Barnabas suggests that Sabbath keeping is impossible. Impossible until the future life in eternity, because in this world all believers are impure and unholy. Barnabas asks, How can we have rest until God's work within our hearts is complete? But in heaven, he states, "we shall be able to treat it [the Sabbath] as holy, after we have first been made holy ourselves."[1]

How sad! To Barnabas, holiness meant perfection of character. He had already forgotten the New Testament truth that being holy simply means being set apart to live for God, not some spiritual attainment. And yet, now I can start growing in grace and begin receiving His power over sin.

Apparently the church was forgetting the gospel through misunderstanding Sabbath rest. Remember, we don't rest in Christ because of our character development but rather because of His accomplishments. The apostle Paul taught that God "has made us accepted in the Beloved" (Ephesians 1:6). "You are complete in Him" (Colossians 2:10). This is the message of the Sabbath.

Had early Christians retained the pure gospel, they never would have forsaken Sabbath rest. Let's explore this further to learn how legalism assisted the Sunday in overtaking the Sabbath.

For Christians in the mid-second century, the main reason for keeping Sunday was that the creation of this world began on the first day of the week, when God made light.

Before long, Christ's resurrection on Sunday became the dominant support for Sunday sacredness. Later on, another reason gained prominence—the fact that the Holy Spirit came to the church on Pentecost Sunday. The Convert's Catechism of Catholic Doctrine,

1977 edition, documents this: "The Church substituted Sunday for Saturday, because Christ rose from the dead on a Sunday, and the Holy Ghost descended upon the Apostles on a Sunday."[2] A favorite verse quoted by church fathers in establishing Sunday sacredness was Malachi 4:2: "But to you who fear My name the Sun of Righteousness shall arise with healing in His wings."

Sunday symbolized spiritual "healing" within the human heart from Jesus, the Sun of righteousness. The process begins when God brings sinners light. Then comes conversion—new life in Christ through His resurrection. Finally the Holy Spirit of Pentecost lives within the believer, restoring the image of God. All these elements of spiritual renewal exist because of events which happened on the first day of the week. One author summarized it this way: "For the Sunday assembly ... [is] a celebration of the re-creation of men." It was regarded as a memorial of God's power to re-create human hearts through the new birth and to subdue sin.

What could be wrong with that? Remember, we are dealing with something subtle here. A sincere error, perhaps, but an error just the same. Something appearing as gospel truth but secretly destroying faith.

Let's go back to Simeon Stylites for a moment, and the problem with Sunday sacredness comes into focus. What was Stylites doing on top of that pillar, fifty feet high in the air? Pursuing sinlessness, spiritual renewal.

Five stories up in the air is pretty high, but not high enough to match the spiritual accomplishments of Jesus. If Simeon Stylites had understood Sabbath rest, he would not have climbed that pillar in the first place. Instead, he would have accepted Christ's perfection as his own accomplishment.

Are you beginning to see what's wrong with Sunday sacredness? It focuses attention on the holiness of the Christian—an imperfect, incomplete ground of hope. The Sabbath, on the other hand, honors the perfect work of Christ done for us. Work pronounced by God to be "very good," done so well that it's finished forever—nothing more can be added to improve it.

Certainly, Christian growth is important. But we cannot confuse what the Bible calls the "fruit" of the gospel—a changed life—with the gospel itself. The gospel, you recall, is the salvation act of God in the death and resurrection of Jesus. The fruit of the gospel is a transformed life because of the indwelling Christ. Do you see the difference?

The Sabbath memorializes the gospel, the finished work of Christ in His life and death. Sunday was made to memorialize the fruit of the gospel, the unfinished work of Christ in our lives. The difference between the two is crucial. Only Sabbath rest provides the assurance that all is well with our souls.

By turning away from Sabbath rest in the completed work of Christ, the church broke the very heart of Christianity. Satan diverted attention from the cross, focusing instead on the imperfect spiritual experience of believers.

## LUTHER AND THE REFORMATION

And so the church plunged into medieval darkness, full of legalism and confusion. A reformation was desperately needed. So God brought Martin Luther on the scene in the 16th century.

Like Simeon Stylites a thousand years earlier, Luther as a young man sought peace and fulfillment by entering a monastery. His pursuit of purity drove him to deprive himself of life's comforts, even its necessities. Some nights, kneeling on the cold stone floor, he would console his conscience, "I have done nothing wrong today." Then doubts would arise: "Am I really pure enough to qualify as a child of God?"

Nothing he could do brought him peace. He could never be certain of satisfying God. But finally he discovered that the peace he was trying so hard to obtain was waiting for him at Calvary's cross. Jesus took the punishment that we sinners deserve, so we could be freely forgiven.

Luther could hardly believe this good news. Despite his guilt he could be counted as perfect, since Jesus, who really was holy, suffered his penalty. He finally realized that believers, though imperfect, can at the same time be counted righteous. God considers sinners to be saints as soon as we trust in Jesus—even before our lives reveal good works (which of course will happen as we grow in Christ).

The conflict between Luther and Rome can be summed up in one verse, Romans 4:5: "To him who does not work but believes on Him who justifies the ungodly, his faith is accounted for righteousness." So the ungodly who entrust themselves to Jesus are justified, forgiven. Forgiveness comes not through our piety. Not by works, Luther learned, but because we put our trust in the life, death, and resurrection of Jesus.

## THE LONG JOURNEY BACK

Half a millennium ago, God commissioned the Lutheran movement to rediscover a neglected truth—the glorious teaching of salvation by faith alone. Luther cleared away the cobwebs of the Dark Ages and restored the foundation of the gospel. But the Reformation wasn't finished with Luther. It had taken centuries of neglect to lose sight of gospel truth, and it would take centuries to restore it.

Is it possible that further light awaits our discovery today as we enter the new millennium? The Bible says: "The path of the just is like the shining sun, that shines ever brighter unto the perfect day" (Proverbs 4:18). So the light of truth will shine brighter, always brighter, until the day of Christ's return. Walking in the light keeps our relationship with God fresh and exciting. There's no danger of getting stale and stagnant when God keeps calling us to move forward in following new truth, stretching us out of our comfort zone into His courageous zone.

How exciting to join the journey toward a full restoration of the truths that Jesus and the apostles believed and taught. We never know what God will be teaching us next! Nevertheless, realizing that He leads only in love, we can always say: "Surely goodness and mercy shall follow me all the days of my life; and I will dwell in the house of the Lord forever" (Psalm 23:6).

## THE SPIRIT OF CASSIE

Now, in closing this chapter, let's go back to Columbine High School. Just two days before the tragedy that ended her life, Cassie Bernall recorded the following testimony on a video for her youth group: "I really can't live without Christ. It's, like, impossible to really have a true life without Him."

Perhaps Cassie remembered those words when she looked down the barrel of a smoking gun. In her supreme test, she backed up her faith with faithfulness.

Jesus said: "Be faithful until death, and I will give you the crown of life" (Revelation 2:10). Cassie Bernall was faithful unto death. She will receive the crown of life.

How about the rest of us? Talk by itself is cheap. Truth is a better test of our faithfulness to God. Will we be faithful, like Cassie, no matter what the cost?

---

1Translation by E. Goodspeed, pp. 40-41; quoted in Samuele Bacchiocchi, *From Sabbath to Sunday,* (Rome: The Pontifical Gregorian University Press, 1977), p. 221.

2Peter Geiermann, *The Convert's Catechism of Catholic Doctrine*, (Rockford, Ill: Tan Books, 1977), p. 50.

# 4 Chapter four
## SECRET OF FATIMA

Vatican City, May 13, 1981. The familiar white Popemobile circles St. Peter's Square amid the waves and cheers of an adoring crowd.

Suddenly gunfire erupts. The shocking news explodes around the world: "The pope has been shot!"

John Paul II survived the assassination attempt and returned to the open arms of a billion Roman Catholics. Exactly one year later he made a pilgrimage to the city of Fatima, Portugal. Surrounded by more than a million celebrants, he thanked the lady of Fatima for saving his life.

Who is this Lady of Fatima? Why does the pope think she saved his life? Is there significance related to Fatima regarding the date of the attempted assassination?

Indeed. On that same date in 1917, three shepherd children were tending their flock around noontime. Suddenly lightning burst through the cloudless sky. The children fled in fear. A beautiful woman materialized in the sky and stopped them. She identified herself as Mary, mother of Christ, commissioned by God to warn the church and the world.

It took six visits to complete and clarify the revelations. Millions of Catholics today, including the pope himself, believe they carry profound prophetic importance as we enter the new millennium.

### INTRIGUING WARNINGS

Most Protestants are surprisingly unaware of these Fatima messages, although they have inspired many books and countless articles. Even an Emmy Award winning film recounts the story of the miraculous revelations. Some Catholic scholars suggest that what happened at Fatima is the most significant spiritual event of the past century.

An amazing assessment. Is it valid? What are these mysterious messages?

First came the prediction that World War I would end. "But if people do not cease offending God, a worse war will break out .... [and God will] punish the world for its crimes by means of war, famine, and persecution of the church and the Holy Father."

Furthermore: "If people do not stop offending God, Russia will spread errors throughout the world, and the good will be martyred. Several nations will be annihilated, but that in the end, Russia will be converted and a certain period of peace will be granted the world."

Then came a third and final secret for the pope alone. No pontiff has ever revealed it publicly, but insiders at the Vatican privately report that it predicts an awful calamity through which God will work to bring the world to repentance. This might be accompanied by an attempt upon the pope's life.

The supernatural messenger promised to return on October 13, 1917, and perform a public miracle to verify the truth of the messages.

Dramatic predictions! Have they come true?

Many newspapers reported that on that very day, an expectant crowd of more than seventy thousand witnessed a miracle in which the sun seemed to gyrate for a full twelve minutes. Other aspects of Fatima's prophecies have been fulfilled beyond question. Russia certainly did become a world power, spreading its atheism around the world. And there was another world war, worse than the first, just as predicted.

Our own generation has seen dramatic events affiliated with Fatima. As noted, the attempted assassination of Pope John Paul II happened on the exact anniversary of the initial appearance to the shepherd children. Also, the fall of Euro-Communism brought Russia many religious opportunities that most Fatima observers believe will lead the way to an eventual Christianization of the country.

So much for the intriguing warnings of Fatima. Who could deny that the world has witnessed dramatic fulfillments? But does that prove God inspired and then orchestrated them?

## WAS IT REALLY MARY?

Back in 1917, a local Roman Catholic priest in Fatima initially suggested that the children, sincere though they were, may have been deceived by a satanic visitation. Was he correct in raising such doubts? Should we scrutinize the source of miraculous occurrences before accepting them as being from God?

Suppose those shepherd children at Fatima really saw a supernatural being. Would this prove it was actually Mary herself appearing miraculously? Remember, Jesus warned earth's final generation that "false prophets will rise and show great signs and wonders to deceive, if possible, even the elect" (Matthew 24:24).

The enemy of our souls is cruel beyond comprehension and incredibly cunning. We can expect dazzling supernatural deceptions in the new millennium. Scripture says: "Beloved, do not believe every spirit, but test the spirits, whether they are of God; because many false prophets have gone out into the world" (1 John 4:1).

So we must test miraculous spirits. By what standard? The Bible! To qualify as from Christ, the messages from Fatima and everything else we believe must synchronize with Scripture.

Over the years since 1917, especially recently, Catholics of all ages and backgrounds have reported many supposed sightings of Mary. Hundreds of them, all over the world. The messages share a common thread. All are urgent calls to repentance and prayer to avoid divine chastisement.

With the world being so wicked, who could argue with a call to repentance? Unfortunately, other elements of these messages raise serious questions.

## MARY HAILED HER SAVIOR

Again and again we hear references to the "immaculate heart" of Mary. Scripture affirms her as a woman of humility and integrity, but was Christ's mother "immaculate" in terms of divine righteousness?

Mary herself acknowledged her need for a personal Savior when she proclaimed: "My soul magnifies the Lord, and my spirit has rejoiced in God my Savior. For He has regarded the lowly state of His maidservant; for behold, henceforth all generations will call me blessed. For He who is mighty has done great things for me, and holy is His name" (Luke 1:46-49).

"God is my Savior," Mary testified. "He has highly favored me, although I don't deserve it." She was "the blessed mother" only because God chose to bless her with unmerited favor. The glory goes to God Himself, not the recipient of His grace.

In Luke 1:35, the angel told the virgin Mary: "The Holy Spirit will come upon you, and the power of the Highest will overshadow you; therefore, also, that Holy One who is to be born will be called the Son of God." Who is "that Holy One"? Jesus. Mary is never described this way in Scripture.

Nevertheless, many suggest that we need Mary as our sinless mediator to approach God. But the Bible teaches: "There is one God and one Mediator between God and men, the Man Christ Jesus" (1 Timothy 2:5). "Let us therefore come boldly to the throne of grace, that we may obtain mercy and find grace to help in time of need" (Hebrews 4:16).

The exaltation of Mary seems almost unbounded. Now there is a worldwide campaign to exalt her to the status of co-redeemer with Jesus. How could this be true, since Christ alone is our salvation?

## CATHOLICS ARE CHRIST-CENTERED?

Despite unauthorized adoration for Mary, most Catholics maintain high regard for Jesus. Protestants often are surprised to learn that their Catholic friends express faith in Christ as their Savior. Let's sample several quotes from the New Catholic Encyclopedia:

"There was, is, and can be only one true way of justification–the gratuitous [free] gift of divine forgiveness offered to man in Christ and received by him in baptismal faith."[1]

And what is faith? "The empty-handed and humble acceptance of the gratuitous gift of divine mercy, forgiveness, and life.... There never was a way of justification by legal works."[2]

"The Christian faith proclaims the fact of man's salvation, which is accomplished by the merciful act of God's love in Christ, who, by means of His life, death, and Resurrection, delivers man from the evil of sin and reunites man in grace with God."[3]

Are our Catholic neighbors really that Christ-centered? Then why did Martin Luther get himself so worked up and worked over if the church already taught a gospel of grace? Let's keep reading:

"This new life is indeed life in Christ, so real that Paul can say, '... It is now no longer I that live, but Christ lives in me.' Thus justification initiates a new life which is a sharing by the Christian in the life of Christ himself."[4]

Fine so far—grace is free and the believer must live in union with Jesus. But soon a yellow caution light starts blinking:

"Sinful man cannot, of himself, be pleasing to God. For that, he must receive a gift from God which transforms him interiorly, cleanses him and sanctifies him by adorning him with qualities that render him pleasing to his Creator. Already, then, we see grace not only as a pure gift of God, which man does not deserve and cannot obtain by himself, but as something which, once given, completely changes him, by purifying him inwardly from sin, and rendering him good and holy."[5]

Do we have a problem here? Certainly sincere Christians surrender themselves to God and commit to live a life that's "good and holy," but the fact remains that we are still unworthy. All of us fall short of God's glorious ideal, the Bible says. "For we all stumble in many things" (James 3:2). Can any one of us look in the mirror and honestly say we are "good and holy" enough to be worthy of heaven? The Bible says that only through the blood of Jesus can God consider us worthy.

The Roman Catholic Church teaches that day by day acceptance with God is not based upon the blood of Jesus, but upon the amount of God's grace reflected in character development. The focus has subtly shifted from the cross to inner holiness attained by the believer. This is a problem. Despite the miracle of transformed lives, "all have sinned and fall short of the glory of God" (Romans 3:23). Certainly grace changes our lives. But there remains that stubborn shortfall that requires the mercy of God. No wonder that the heart of the gospel is God's grace—His completely undeserved gift of salvation provided to all who are willing to humble themselves by confessing themselves as sinners and then believing that Jesus died on their behalf as their Savior. Then God raised Him from the dead and brought Him up to heaven as proof that His sacrifice for our salvation is acceptable in the judgment.

## HALFWAY HOUSE TO HEAVEN?

Meet Cathy, a thirtysomething Christian raised as a devout Catholic to love Jesus and also adore the saints. While she was a teenager, a favorite book was the fifteenth century devotional classic Imitation of Christ, familiar to Catholics everywhere. She loved to meditate on excerpts such as this:

"St. Lawrence, through the love of God overcame mightily the love of the world and of himself. He despised all that was pleasant and delectable in the world.... Do in like manner, and learn to forsake some necessary and some well-beloved friend for the love of God."[6]

Cathy admired this saint for loving God rather than the world, but she wondered why he had to reject everything pleasant—even innocent friendships. Nevertheless, inspired by such sentiments, she determined to devote her life to religious service and take the vows of poverty, chastity and obedience. As it turned out, she fell in love and got married. Still she remained a faithful Roman Catholic.

In catechism classes, Cathy had learned this version of the gospel: "I can't save myself. By faith, however, I can receive the free gift of God's life-changing grace through Jesus Christ. His grace changes my heart to make me worthy."

The haunting question, of course, is How worthy must one become to be good enough to be saved?

This mattered to Cathy because she really cares about God. Despite her demanding responsibilities as the mother of several children, she would never miss a mass or confession. She saved and sacrificed to send her children to parochial schools. Her priest considered her an exemplary daughter of the church.

Privately, however, Cathy suffered severe guilt, like a toothache that never goes away. This feeling of sinfulness wasn't from anything particular she was doing wrong. It was a vague sense of not doing enough to please God. She discussed this with her priest, who assured her that she was a wonderful mother and shouldn't scold herself for not being able to help the homeless more or do whatever else her restless conscience demanded. Even so, Cathy had an indefinable but powerful sense of coming up short before God, not being close enough to Him, not having enough of Jesus in her life, or the graces of His Spirit.

Lacking assurance about salvation, Cathy was afraid of purgatory. She understood it as sort of a halfway house on the way to heaven where her character could be cleansed to perfection. She worried about how many centuries of suffering she would need to endure before finally becoming worthy of entering God's presence.

Progressive Catholics now suggest that purgatory may not involve actual physical suffering. It's more like being stuck during February in a Chicago snowstorm. You'd rather be surfing in Hawaii, but at least you're not starving in a Siberian gulag.

Cathy welcomed the idea of a new and improved purgatory, kinder and gentler than the nasty place she had heard about all her life. Yet she still wished she could just go directly to heaven instead of suffering any time of separation from Jesus.

Then she made the same discovery Martin Luther did five centuries ago. Every Christian already is worthy of heaven. By Christ's death and resurrection He "qualified us to be partakers of the inheritance of the saints" (Colossians 1:12). No need for purgatory! "For by one offering He has perfected forever those who are being sanctified" (Hebrews 10:14).

"Fantastic!" Cathy exclaimed. "God considers me perfect already, here and now—despite my struggles and failures! Thanks to Jesus, I'm a saint here and now already worthy of heaven!"

Cathy sees special significance in those words: "by one offering." The church had taught her that every time she went to mass there was yet another sacrifice for her sin. Not so, she now knows. Jesus on the cross proclaimed with His dying breath: "It is finished!" (John 19:30). His one sacrifice for sin is good for all time and eternity.

Cathy now attends a church where celebrating Holy Communion is a memorial of Christ's finished work, not an endless repetition of what He already finished for all time; much like her marriage anniversary, an ongoing memorial of her wedding, which was a once-for-all-time event.

## THE DISAPPEARING COMMANDMENT

Cathy's new understanding of the gospel changed her attitude toward images of Mary and other saints. Not that she ever had worshiped the images themselves. She knew they were but statues of wood and stone, but they served to remind her of God's perfection in His people. She thought she was ultimately worshiping God by adoring the saints and their images. Finally she understood that Christ alone is worthy, and she is just as much a saint as anyone else who ever lived.

One day she read something in Scripture that caused her to clear her home of all statues associated with worship. It was the Ten Commandments, the second of which warns: "You shall not make for yourself a carved image, or any likeness of anything that is in heaven above, or that is in the earth beneath, or that is in the water under the earth; you shall not bow down to them nor serve them. For I, the Lord your God, am a jealous God" (Exodus 20:4-5).

Cathy had never read this before, even though catechism classes had thoroughly focused on the Ten Commandments, one by one. Somehow this particular commandment was omitted. Why?

Evidently church leaders felt uncomfortable with a commandment forbidding the use of images in worship, so they simply discarded it. Then how did they still come up with 10 commandments? By splitting the tenth into two. (And then, you recall, they also attempted to change the fourth commandment, abolishing the seventh-day Sabbath.)

The background of this is fascinating. Let's go back to 16th century Italy and the Council of Trent, a landmark event in the history of Roman Catholicism. Church leaders reacting against the Protestant Reformation reaffirmed the use of images in worship. Curiously, this same council also emphasized the importance of obedience to God's Ten Commandments by voting a series of powerful statements. Notice several of them:

"18. If anyone says that the commandments of God are impossible to observe even for a man who is justified and in the state of grace: let him be anathema.

"19. If anyone says that ... the Ten Commandments do not pertain at all to Christians: let him be anathema.

"21. If anyone says that God has given Jesus Christ to men as a redeemer in whom they are to trust, but not as a lawgiver whom they are to obey: let him be anathema."[7]

Catholic leaders at Trent also expressed confidence that God would provide power to perfectly fulfil His commandments: "For unless men are unfaithful to his grace, God will bring the good work to perfection, just as he began it, working both the will and the performance."[8]

Throughout their history, Catholics have expressed commitment to God's commandments. Consider their respect for morality in both heart and home. How shocking and incongruous that they have broken the Ten Commandments by abolishing one and changing another! But these particular changes were not accidental. Significantly, both alterations to God's law undermine the gospel of His grace. The second commandment withholds honor from anyone but God Himself, for He alone is holy and worthy; the fourth commandment with its Sabbath rest memorializes Christ's finished work, in which we find the gift of salvation.

Where did the church get authority to tamper with God's law and subvert the gospel? Not in Scripture. Obviously tradition supplanted truth, as in the time of Jesus. He had warned the priests of His day: "Laying aside the commandment of God, you hold the tradition of men. ... You reject the commandment of God, that you may keep your tradition" (Mark 7:8-9). He solemnly concluded: "In vain they worship Me, teaching as doctrines the commandments of men" (verse 9).

Vain worship–quite a warning! In the Bible, even angels from heaven admonished those who tried to worship them to instead "Worship God" (Revelation 19:10; 22:9). There is a word in Scripture that describes exalting any human to a place where only God belongs. That solemn word is blasphemy (see John 10:33). God understands when people all their lives have sincerely worshiped Mary as "Queen of Heaven." "Truly, these times of ignorance God overlooked, but now commands all men everywhere to repent" (Acts 17:30).

## TRUTH IS THE TEST

What about the miracles associated with worshiping Mary? To be consistent with Scripture, anything supernatural associated with blasphemous worship must be "according to the working of Satan, with all power, signs, and lying wonders" (2 Thessalonians 2:9).

Devilish deceptions. "And no wonder! For Satan himself transforms himself into an angel of light. Therefore it is no great thing if his ministers also transform themselves into ministers of righteousness, whose end will be according to their works" (2 Corinthians 11:14-15). The great deceiver will impersonate departed saints, angels–even Christ Himself. He can do miracles in the sky, such as making the sun appear to spin as it did at Fatima.

You may have seen the bumper sticker: Expect a Miracle! Praise God, He does work miracles. Let's just remember, so does the enemy. Jesus told the miracle-minded crowds who followed Him: "Not everyone who says to Me, 'Lord, Lord,' shall enter the kingdom of heaven, but he who does the will of My Father in heaven. Many will say to Me in that day, 'Lord, Lord, have we not prophesied in Your name, cast out demons in Your name, and done many wonders in Your name?' And then I will declare to them, 'I never knew you; depart from Me, you who practice lawlessness!'" (Matthew 7:21-23).

Incredible! People will speak in Christ's name, perform miracles of healing, and even apparently cast out demons–yet be empowered by the devil. So how may we know God has not sent them? Lawlessness is one dead giveaway. If they reject any of God's commandments, their claim to represent Christ is counterfeit.

"Now by this we know that we know Him, if we keep His commandments. He who says, 'I know Him,' and does not keep His commandments, is a liar, and the truth is not in him" (1 John 2:3-4).

The miracles of millennimania are no proof of God's presence and power. Bible truth is the proof.

---

[1] *The New Catholic Encyclopedia*, (New York: McGraw & Hill, 1967), VIII, p. 79. Hereafter cited as Catholic Encyclopedia.

[2] *Catholic Encyclopedia*, VIII, pp. 79, 80.

[3] *Catholic Encyclopedia*, XIII, p. 444.

[4] P. Gregory Stephens, OSB, *The Life of Grace*, (Washington, D.C.: Catholic University of America, 1963), p. 33.

[5] Jean Daujat, *The Theology of Grace*, (London: Burns & Oates, 1959), p. 14.

[6] Thomas a Kempis, *The Imitation of Christ*, by (New York: Doubleday, 1955), p. 87.

[7] John F. Clarkson, et al, *The Church Teaches*, (Rockford, IL: Tan Books & Publishers, 1973), p. 244.

[8] Clarkson, *Church*, p. 238.

# 5. Chapter five
## THE MEDIEVAL ANTICHRIST

The year was 1517. Life was bleak in medieval Germany. Then a little excitement came to town. Johann Tetzel showed up with salvation for sale.

With bells pealing and children shouting, he paraded through the gates and planted the papal banner in the town square. Tetzel held the exclusive regional franchise for selling "indulgences," which guaranteed fire insurance against punishment in purgatory, plus release for poor souls already suffering there.

Posting the pope's authorization on a background of red and gold velvet, Tetzel got down to business. The carnival spirit waned somewhat as he launched into a spine-chilling description of souls writhing in purgatory. Then, pointing to the stack of indulgences beside him, he climaxed his sales pitch: "As the coin in the coffer rings, so the soul from purgatory springs."

Tetzel's poetic flair wasn't Billy Graham's style, yet many came forward and purchased pardons. Martin Luther, looking on, was not impressed by the promotion and pageantry. "I'll knock a hole in his drum," he declared.

He did more than that, and the world has never been the same.

First Luther took his pen and authored a powerful series of objections to the peddling of pardons. Then he grabbed a hammer and nailed those Ninety-five Theses to the heavy wooden door of Wittenberg's cathedral. They sparkled in Luther's trademark style—courageous, concise and compelling.

"Saints have no extra credits," he thundered. "And Christ's merits are freely available. ... If the pope does have power to release anyone from purgatory, why in the name of love does he not abolish purgatory by letting everyone out?"

Luther defied anyone to debate him. Copies of his theses stormed Europe. Although his goal was reform, not revolt, Rome pronounced him a rebel and heretic. The pope warned him to recant or face church punishment. The reformer resolved to press forward. He acclaimed Jesus as the only true mediator for sinners, accusing the church of interfering with a believer's personal relationship with God.

He asserted: "The true Christian pilgrimage is not to Rome, ... but to the prophets, the Psalms and the Gospels."

Yet incredibly, when Catholic scholar Erasmus translated the New Testament from Latin into the language of the people, church leaders in Rome officially condemned God's Word on its "Index of Forbidden Books." Imagine!

In Luther's time, politics had displaced piety. Spiritual confusion abounded. Not long before, three rival church leaders at the same time had claimed to be pope, with each condemning the others as being the dreaded antichrist. Luther said that they all had been correct and that church system itself had become the antichrist power.

The Reformer's uncompromising stand separated him from Rome. The divorce became final when Luther officially condemned the papal power as antichrist. Pope Leo X returned the favor with a declaration of excommunication on January 3, 1521. He banned Luther's writings, ordering them to be burned. Luther himself seemed bound for the flames.

In our day, many suggest that Luther was hyperventilating in the heat of battle when he announced that the church had become the antichrist's headquarters. But this was no rash statement against the medieval religious system. Rome was waging war against God's truth, persecuting anyone courageous enough to proclaim the Bible alone as the foundation of teaching and grace alone through faith alone as the basis of salvation. In fact, all Reformers pointed fearless fingers toward Rome, including John Knox of Scotland, and even King James I, who commissioned our King James Bible. So did Sir Isaac Newton, renowned scientist and student of Scripture. All arrived at that conclusion reluctantly through careful Bible study.

Were they correct in their assessment of the medieval church? Let's do a reality check on the Protestant Reformation. First we need some background on the meaning of the word antichrist.

## SUBTLE OPPOSITION

"Let no one deceive you by any means; for that Day [the second coming of Christ] will not come unless the falling away comes first, and the man of sin is revealed, the son of perdition" (2 Thessalonians 2:3). This "man of sin" is universally understood as the antichrist power. It would emerge amid a "falling away" or apostasy within the Christian church itself.

Incredible! Did this really happen? Tragically, yes. Pagan ceremonies and holy days infiltrated the church and soon became enshrined as Christian traditions. Many believers who stood firmly against persecution let pagan influences taint their faith. Church leadership compromised the gospel, and Christianity in general suffered a serious loss of faith.

Should this surprise us? After all, had not God's people throughout Old Testament history continually wandered from the covenant? Besides, as we saw a few pages ago, the New Testament predicted the apostasy. Let's probe deeper now.

Paul said the "falling away" would originate within the church (2 Thessalonians 2:3), adding the stunning revelation: "the mystery of lawlessness is already at work" (verse 7). So the seeds of apostasy existed in the first century. Even as the New Testament was being written, the antichrist power had already begun to function. It would prosper and grow throughout the long centuries until taking its final form just before Christ's coming.

Future chapters will focus on prophecies of the antichrist's final work before Jesus comes. For now, let's see how this deceptive force has been operating throughout the last two millennia. To begin, we need some background on the meaning of the word antichrist.

The Greek word translated anti in antichrist can mean either "against" or "instead of." So the antichrist power is not necessarily some openly atheistic power openly opposed to Christ. Rather, it might assume for itself titles and roles that belong exclusively to Jesus, all the while giving Him lip service. That would be subtle and extremely deceptive, like the wolf in sheep's clothing Jesus warned about.

Which of those two strategies would the devil employ in his attack upon truth? No need to guess. Bible prophecy warns regarding the antichrist: "Let no man deceive you." There's nothing deceptive about an outright attack on Christianity. Instead, the antichrist power would position itself in Christ's place, seeming to respect His divine role while subverting His authority. Is this happening when the church puts its saints between the sinner and the Savior—when the

Bible says there is just "one mediator between God and man, the Man Christ Jesus" (1 Timothy 2:5)? And what about when the church exalts Mary as "Queen of Heaven" when the Bible gives all celestial honor to God alone? How about purgatory, which denies the truth that "there is therefore now no condemnation to those who are in Christ Jesus" (Romans 8:1)?

All of those teachings of the church contradict Christian faith, and the Bible says, "Whatever is not from faith is sin" (Romans 14:23). And how about when the church assumes for itself authority to change heaven's holy law? The antichrist, or "man of sin," doesn't need to attack all ten of God's commandments, by promoting adultery, lying and stealing. No honest seeker of truth would be deceived by such strategy. The "man of sin" works deception by claiming to uphold the Ten Commandments while voiding two of them. And God considers an attack on just one commandment as a war against them all (see James 2:10).

Just as the Scripture foretold, the antichrist did emerge amid a "falling away" or apostasy within the Christian church itself. Shocking and sad, yet it's just as God predicted.

## DANIEL'S ANCIENT PROPHECY

Now let's explore an Old Testament prophecy that convinced the Reformers about the antichrist. Daniel chapter 7 records the fascinating prediction. It's a prophecy concerning four beasts, or kingdoms. Verse 23 explains that "the fourth beast shall be the fourth kingdom on earth, which shall be different from all other kingdoms."

Scholars agree that the four kingdoms of Daniel 7 are Babylon, Greece, Persia and Rome. And this text predicted that the fourth kingdom, the Roman empire, would be different from the other three. Rather than giving way to another single world power, Rome would be followed by ten kingdoms. Notice: "The ten horns are ten kings who shall arise from this kingdom. And another shall arise after them; he shall be different from the first ones, and shall subdue three kings" (Daniel 7:24).

Did the Roman empire indeed collapse into a coalition of ten kingdoms? Indeed. Modern Europe descended from ten Germanic tribes which followed the Roman empire. And our text predicted that three of those tribes would succumb to a new power headquartered in Rome–a religious and political coalition that eventually developed into the Holy Roman Empire. It's fascinating to recall how this happened.

In the early fourth century, the Roman empire was sagging with age. Threats loomed both within and beyond its borders. Confronted with steady problems, the Emperor Constantine converted to Christianity–a remarkable development, given the hostility that previous rulers of the empire had shown to the church. He quickly launched a campaign to Christianize his kingdom.

Problems persisted, however. Seeking escape from economic headaches and the threat of invasion from barbarian tribes, the emperor relocated eight hundred miles east. Constantinople (now Istanbul, Turkey) became his capital. From that time forward, the Roman church dominated the western empire.

So history confirms the prediction that a religious power in Rome would succeed its secular leadership. A popular college textbook certifies this transfer of power from the Roman empire to the Roman church:

"In the West, the Church took over the defense of Roman civilization. The emperor gave up the [pagan] title of Pontifiex Maximus (high priest) because the Roman gods were no longer worshiped. The bishop of Rome assumed these priestly functions, and this is why the Pope today is sometimes referred to as the Pontiff. ... The Roman Empire had become the Christian Church."[1]

When the Huns, a fierce and savage tribe led by brutal Attila, swept into Italy and threatened to take and destroy the city of Rome, it was the leader of the Christian Church, Pope Leo, not the emperor, who met the barbarian. Attila was so impressed with the Pope's spiritual power that he turned back. What Leo said to Attila remains unknown, but what is significant is the fact that it was the Pope and not the emperor who stood at the gates of Rome.

Rome eventually fell to the barbarian tribes–ten of them, just as Daniel 7 had predicted a millennium beforehand. The church, however, managed to Christianize the invaders, thus maintaining its control of the western empire. What about the three tribes that resisted papal authority?

In 533 the Emperor Justinian officially declared the pope to be"head of all the holy churches." In harmony with this declaration he waged war on anyone who refused to honor the authority of the church. Three of the ten tribes–the Herulis, the Ostrogoths and the Vandals–refused to submit to the papacy. But in March of 538 the last of those rebel tribes fell and the pope reigned supreme over Christendom.

So ten kingdoms followed Rome. And three of them fell to make way for the papacy. Just a coincidence, or a striking fulfillment of the prophecy that he "shall subdue three kings"? (Daniel 7:24).

## FOUR ADDITIONAL MARKS OF THE ANTICHRIST

Daniel 7 went on to predict that "he shall speak pompous words against the Most High, and shall persecute the saints of the Most High, and shall intend to change times and law. Then the saints shall be given unto his hand for a time and times and half a time" (verse 25).

Did these things really happen in the church? We'll know after considering those four identifying marks, one by one:

### 1 ) "HE SHALL SPEAK POMPOUS WORDS AGAINST THE MOST HIGH"

The church claimed authority to dispense God's forgiveness. In 1076 Pope Gregory VII declared that the citizens of Germany need not obey their king until he submitted to papal authority. Henry IV, most powerful monarch in Europe, hurried over the wintery Alps to Canossa where the pontiff was residing. There he shivered barefoot in the snow for three days, waiting until the pope finally forgave him.

Quite a remarkable encounter between church and state. The medieval popes even claimed authority over personal conscience. And in the late 19th century Pope Leo VII commanded "complete submission and obedience of will to the Church and to the Roman Pontiff, as to God Himself."[2] Four years later he made the bold claim: "We [the popes] hold upon this earth the place of God Almighty."[3]

It is not for us to question anyone's sincerity. But requiring allegiance due to God alone ventures onto dangerous ground.

### 2) HE "SHALL PERSECUTE THE SAINTS OF THE MOST HIGH"

The church today frankly acknowledges its history of persecution. According to the New Catholic Encyclopedia, "In 1252

[Pope] Innocent IV sanctioned the infliction of torture by the civil authorities upon heretics, and torture came to have a recognized place in the procedure of the inquisitorial courts."[4]

After venting on the Muslims, Jews, and even fellow Christians of the Eastern Orthodox communion, Rome turned its sword against Christian "heretics" in Europe. During those dark centuries, fearful crusades brought wrath upon the Albigenses in southern France and other Christian nonconformists. Many thousands died for their beliefs by being hung, drowned or burned alive. The record of history is open for all to read.

August 23, 1572, was perhaps the darkest hour of the church. A bell tolling in the middle of the night signaled the start of the Massacre of Saint Bartholomew in France. Soldiers dragged unsuspecting Protestants from their beds, into the dark streets, and slaughtered them as children screamed in terror.

For days the bloodbath continued in Paris and the surrounding provinces. Noble and peasant, old and young, mother and child spilled their blood together. Only heaven knows how many perished in this medieval holocaust—as many as seventy thousand, according to some sources.[5]

When news of the bloodbath reached Rome, the city erupted in celebration. Church bells rang. The cannon of St. Angelo thundered a joyous salute. Pope Gregory XIII had a medallion minted to commemorate the horrors of the Massacre.

Catholics today regret those tragic events. We all must resist condemning medieval church leaders for these atrocities. How much better to pray with Christ, "Father forgive them, for they know not what they do."

So the persecuting Inquisitions and Crusades came in the name of the cross of Christ. Interestingly, the word "crusade" comes from the Latin word for "cross." Crusaders wore a red cloth cross sewn on their tunics to show they were Christian soldiers. The medieval church believed that carrying the cross of Christ meant killing nonconformists.

But is the cross of Jesus a sword? Our Lord never led an army. In the garden of Gethsemane He told Peter to put the sword away. Jesus then warned that those who take up the sword would perish by the sword.

Evidently the medieval church had lost sight of true Christianity. Pure gospel faith became buried beneath tradition, legalism and a persecution policy. The church through its use of force and fear violated God's covenant of grace. Indeed, "judged by contemporary standards, the Inquisition, especially as it developed in Spain toward the close of the Middle Ages, can be classified only as one of the darker chapters in the history of the Church."[6]

## 3) HE "SHALL INTEND TO CHANGE TIMES AND LAW"

Has the church attempted to change the Ten Commandments, specifically in regard to time? We saw this in our last chapter. In fact, it became official church policy.

Around the year 1400, Petrus de Ancharano declared that "the pope can modify divine law, since his power is not of man, but of God, and he acts in the place of God on earth."[7] Martin Luther vigorously disputed this teaching of the church. In the reformer's famous debate with the papal representative Johann Eck, he affirmed that no church tradition would rule his life. Only the Holy Scriptures had control over his conscience.

But Dr. Eck had a card up his sleeve. He called Luther to account for keeping Sunday in place of the Bible Sabbath. Here is his challenge to the reformer:

"Scripture teaches, 'Remember to hallow the Sabbath day; six days shall you labor and do all your work, but the seventh day is the Sabbath day of the Lord your God,' etc. Yet the church has changed the Sabbath into Sunday on its own authority, on which you have no Scripture."[8]

Eck had a point which Luther could not deny. In his battle against church tradition the reformer had not yet come to grips with the Sabbath question.

The Roman Catholic Church today acknowledges the origin of Sunday keeping. This revealing quote is from The Convert's Catechism of Catholic Doctrine (1977 ed.):

"Q. Which is the Sabbath day?

"A. Saturday is the Sabbath day.

"Q. Why do we observe Sunday instead of Saturday.

"A. We observe Sunday instead of Saturday because the Catholic Church transferred the solemnity from Saturday to Sunday."[9]

Fascinating. We also read in the contemporary best-seller, The Faith of Millions:

"Since Saturday, not Sunday, is specified in the Bible, isn't it curious that non-Catholics who profess to take their religion directly from the Bible and not from the Church, observe Sunday instead of Saturday? ... That observance remains as a reminder of the Mother Church from which the non-Catholic sects broke away–like a boy running away from home but still carrying in his pocket a picture of his mother or a lock of her hair."[10]

Perhaps Protestants ought to ask themselves why they keep Sunday, since tradition accounts for its origin.

Here's the point: When it comes to Sabbath versus Sunday, the church fulfils Daniel 7 by claiming authority to change "times and law." And now, one last test remains before we can positively identify the Holy Roman Empire as the fulfillment of Daniel's prophecy.

## 4) "THE SAINTS SHALL BE GIVEN INTO HIS HAND FOR A TIME AND TIMES AND HALF A TIME"

What prophetic time span do we have here? The reformers understood these three and a half times to represent 1260 years of papal authority. How did they figure this?

Here in Daniel 7 they found these three and a half times, and they noticed that in Revelation 13:5 this same time span is spoken of as 42 months. Then again in Revelation 12:6 as 1260 days.

Are these 1260 days literal or symbolic? It helps to know that in Bible prophecy short-lived beasts symbolize centuries of government. So a much longer time span than 1260 literal days is called for. The answer comes when we realize that in symbolic prophecy a day represents a year (see Ezekiel 4:6).

Now we can see why the reformers interpreted these 1260 days as 1260 years. As far back as the late 12th century, the Catholic scholar Joachim of Flores, summoned to answer charges of heresy, declared that these 1260 days represented 1260 years of power in the church.[11] And way back in the ninth century several students of the Word believed the same.[12]

History confirms their scholarship. Remember A.D. 538, the year when the last rebel tribe was crushed? It so happened that exactly 1260 years later, in 1798, that Napoleon's army stormed the Vatican. They captured Pope Pius IV and took him into exile, where he died. A most remarkable and dramatic fulfillment of Bible prophecy!

## COUNTERING THE REFORMATION

Back in the sixteenth century, the pope increasingly felt threatened by the Protestant Reformation. And so, to meet the challenge, he summoned church leaders to the Council of Trent. Church leaders not only reaffirmed their basic beliefs, they also took the offensive by launching the Counter-Reformation. Through political manipulation, military force and the incredibly cruel persecutions of the Inquisition, Rome regained large territories lost to the Protestants.

The Jesuits, a new religious order, implemented the Counter-Reformation. They trained tirelessly and served sacrificially in their assignment of reversing the Reformation. Two of their best scholars, Luis de Alcazar and Francisco Ribera, confronted the most explosive charge of the Protestants–that the church of Rome had become the antichrist.

Alcazar suggested that the prophecies regarding antichrist had been fulfilled in the past with pagan Rome, before the popes had power. His position became known as preterism. Ribera taught the opposite view, futurism. He said the antichrist would arise in power only in the last days. Either way, whether the antichrist was past or future, the Jesuits had achieved their goal. They had taken the heat off the pope.

How did Ribera manage to relegate into the far-off future the prophecies concerning the antichrist? By skillfully manipulating that beautiful prophecy in Daniel 9, which foretold the year of Christ's death. Ribera took the heart out of Daniel 9 by replacing Christ with the antichrist. (If you recall, we noted this in chapter two.)

Predictably, Protestants rejected Roman Catholic futurism. Of two dozen major Reformation scholars between 1639 and the end of the seventeenth century, every one still referred to the antichrist as the papacy. They also maintained their faith that Jesus had fulfilled the seventy weeks prophecy of Daniel.

But incredibly, Protestants in the last two centuries have abandoned the prophetic faith of their founders by adopting and adapting the futurism of the Jesuits! Of all the surprises in the development of Christian teaching, what can surpass this? George Eldon Ladd, an honored scholar of our day, documents it in his book The Blessed Hope:

"It will probably come as a shock to many modern futurists to be told that the first scholar in relatively modern times who returned to the patristic futuristic interpretation was a Spanish Jesuit named Ribera. In 1590, Ribera published a commentary on the Revelation as a counter-interpretation to the prevailing view among Protestants which identified the Papacy with the antichrist. Ribera applied all of Revelation but the earliest chapters to the end time rather than to the history of the Church. Antichrist would be a single evil person who would be received by the Jews and would rebuild Jerusalem, abolish Christianity, deny Christ, persecute the Church and rule the world for three and a half years."[13]

## AUTOPSY OF APOSTASY

Evidently, Protestants have suffered a serious loss of their prophetic heritage. How did this apostasy happen?

To get the story, we must cross the Atlantic and go back to the early 1830's. Edward Irving, a pastor of the Church of Scotland, became fascinated by the predictions of Christ's second coming and co-founded the Society for the Investigation of Prophecy. Unfortunately, he accepted Ribera's futurism and even translated the book of a Spanish Jesuit scholar.

Irving captured the interest of London's high society as well as the populace. In Scotland, he taught an outdoor audience of twelve thousand. Although Irving died in middle age, his influence survived and thrived. Through his teaching, Irish Anglican John Nelson Darby adopted Ribera's futurism. This zealous young man journeyed around Europe and the United States proclaiming his beliefs. When he died in 1882, Darby could number nearly one hundred study groups in America committed to his prophetic interpretations.

After Darby, the torch of futurism passed to C. I. Scofield, compiler of the study notes in the Scofield Reference Bible. First published in 1909, Scofield's Bible remains quite popular today.

Since 1970, Hal Lindsey's best-seller The Late Great Planet Earth has influenced millions of Protestants to accept a futurist view of the antichrist.

Incredible but true–Protestants themselves welcomed with open arms a diversionary teaching of Rome's Counter-Reformation. No wonder so much confusion exists about Bible prophecy. Those who share the spirit of the Reformation may well feel concerned that so many Protestants have forfeited their prophetic faith for the deceptions of futurism with its medieval roots.

## HIGH COST OF IGNORANCE

After learning all that, some simply shrug their shoulders: "What difference does it make what we believe about the antichrist, so long as we sincerely believe in the real Jesus?" If we really are that sincere, will we not take His Word seriously with its warnings about prophetic deceptions?

During Christ's ministry on earth, misconceptions about Bible prophecy led many to reject Him. They looked for a Messiah who would chase out the Roman occupation force. When Jesus just healed the sick and raised the dead, He didn't fit their job description.

None other than faithful and fearless John the Baptist became confused. He dispatched a delegation of his disciples to Jesus asking: "Are You the Coming One, or do we look for another?" (Matthew 11:3).

Similar doubts and delusions overcame the whole nation. This confusion climaxed toward the end of Christ's ministry. In John 7 we see Jesus in Jerusalem attending the Feast of Tabernacles. "There was much murmuring among the people concerning Him. Some said, 'He is good'; others said, 'No, on the contrary, He deceives the people'" (John 7:11-12).

The debate about Jesus swept back and forth. Once again a popular misconception of Bible prophecy caused Christ's hearers to question His identity. They murmured: "We know where this Man is from; but when the Christ comes, no one knows where He is from" (verse 27).

Evidently many believed that Messiah would show up suddenly and mysteriously out of nowhere. Since Jesus had been around awhile, they didn't think He qualified for consideration. Their total ignorance of prophecy caused them to shun their Savior.

Others knew more about the Bible but still rejected Jesus. Realizing that Messiah would be born in Bethlehem—as Jesus indeed was—they objected to His hometown of Nazareth: "'Will the Christ come out of Galilee? Has not the Scripture said that the Christ comes from the seed of David and from the town of Bethlehem, where David was?' So there was a division among the people because of Him" (John 7:41-43).

A little background check would have resolved their perplexity. Bible prophecy had called for Messiah to live in Nazareth after His birth in Bethlehem (see Matthew 2:23). But misinformation led thousands to reject Jesus.

Actually, false information about prophecy can be worse than no information at all. People imagine themselves knowledgeable when they are tragically mistaken.

Multitudes in Christ's day didn't bother studying the Bible for themselves. All they cared about was: "Have any of the rulers or the Pharisees believed on Him?" (John 7:48). "Does anybody famous agree with what God is teaching me? I'm not going to follow truth until my favorite religious celebrity leads the way."

Do we still hear echoes of that attitude today?

You know the sad ending back in Jesus' time on earth. He failed Israel's expectations, so they failed to accept Him—all because of their unwillingness to examine the prophecies with an open mind and teachable attitude.

Are we in similar danger today? Remember Paul's warning about the antichrist: "Let no one deceive you by any means" (2 Thessalonians 2:3). Perhaps we are scouting the horizon for some future pagan antichrist power when all the time it has been flourishing within Christianity.

Something to think about carefully.

Blinded by spiritual millennimania, will some unknowing Christians even cooperate with the antichrist's deceptions? A haunting but plausible possibility.

There's too much to lose in earth's last hours to allow ourselves be ignorant, or to take someone else's word about what is Bible truth.

God can help us study the Scriptures for ourselves and then follow its sure word of prophecy.

[1] Harry A. Dawe, *Ancient Greece and Rome: World Cultures in Perspective* (Columbus, Ohio: Charles E. Merrill, 1970), p. 188. Italics supplied.

[2] Encyclical letter "Chief Duties of Christians," January 10, 1890. Cited by C. Mervyn Maxwell, *God Cares*, (Boise, Id.: Pacific Press Publishing Association, 1981) vol. 1, p.131.

[3] "The Reunion of Christendom," dated June 20, 1894. Cited by Maxwell, *God Cares*, vol. 1, p. 131.

[4] "Torture," *Catholic Encyclopedia.*

[5] "Huguenots," in *Grolier's Academic American Encyclopedia,* electronic edition, estimates a St. Bartholomew's slaughter of between 30,000 and 70,000.

[6] "Inquisition," *Catholic Encyclopedia.*

[7] See Lucius Ferraris, *Prompta Bibliotheca*, 8 vols. (Venice: Caspa Storti, 1772), article "Papa, II." Cited in Maxwell, *God Cares*, vol. 1, p. 134.

[8] Johann Eck, *Enchiridion of Commonplaces of John Eck Against Luther and Other Enemies of the Church*, trans. F. L. Battles, 2d ed. (Grand Rapids, Mich.: Calvin Theological Seminary, 1978), vol. 8, p. 13. Cited in Maxwell, *God Cares*, vol. 1, p. 134.

[9] Peter Geiermann, *The Convert's Catechism of Catholic Doctrine,* (Rockford, Ill: Tan Books, 1977), p. 50.

[10] John A. O'Brien, *The Faith of Millions,* (Huntington, Ind: Our Sunday Visitor, 1974), pp. 400, 401.

[11] LeRoy Froom, *The Prophetic Faith of Our Fathers*, (Washington: Review & Herald, 1954), vol. 1, p. 713.

[12] *Ibid.*

[13] George Eldon Ladd, *The Blessed Hope,* (Grand Rapids, Mich.: Eerdmans Publishing Co., 1956), pp. 37, 38.

# Chapter six

## HOW THE EAST WAS WON

"Mr. Gorbachev, open this gate! Mr. Gorbachev, tear down this wall!"

It was a landmark moment in the long Cold War between the superpowers. The year was 1987. The place was West Berlin.

As the huge crowd cheered, U.S. President Ronald Reagan challenged Soviet leader Mikhail Gorbachev to let freedom reign. He was calling for a new world order, with the collapse of Euro-Communism to the east. And against all odds and appearances, it happened.

The president's spine-tingling speech inspired the free world, but few dared hope for results, at least not in that millennium. Few, that is, besides Reagan himself and Pope John Paul II. They shared a vision of abolishing the evil empire of Soviet atheism. As the two most powerful men in the West, they also had limitless resources to support and implement their bold campaign. And they were fiercely motivated. Both, having barely escaped death through assassination, believed God had spared their lives to overthrow Communism.

A leading Cardinal and close aid to the pope recalled: "In their first meeting, the Holy Father and the President committed themselves and the institutions of the church and America to such a goal. And from that day, the focus was to bring it about in Poland." Together they developed a secret strategy to topple the Soviet stranglehold. Major players in this behind-the-scenes drama were a half dozen high officials in U.S. government, led by CIA chief William Casey. All of them were devout Roman Catholics. Many mornings they sipped Italian cappuccino at the home of the Vatican ambassador to the United States, brainstorming and coordinating their efforts. The pope and the president provided continual direction and received day by day progress reports.

Organized labor in the United States, Sweden and Poland played a crucial role in the grand scheme. The CIA and AFL-CIO shipped broadcasting equipment, computers, and fax machines to Scandinavia. There they were repackaged and smuggled by ship into the Polish port of Gdansk. Dock workers unloaded the huge crates in plain view of unsuspecting customs inspectors. From storage warehouses, the contents were loaded into vans and distributed throughout Poland through a network of church workers and Solidarity leaders.

The electronic gadgetry found good use. In church basements and homes, millions viewed documentary videos produced and displayed on the contraband equipment. More than four hundred underground publications appeared out of nowhere, some with a circulation exceeding thirty thousand. Books and pamphlets debunking communist propaganda and confronting the government surfaced everywhere.

As reported in Time magazine, "With clandestine broadcasting equipment, ... Solidarity regularly broke into the government's radio programming, often with the message 'Solidarity lives!' or 'Resist!' Armed with a transmitter supplied by the CIA through church channels, Solidarity interrupted television programming with both audio and visual messages, including calls for strikes and demonstrations. 'There was a great moment at the half time of the national soccer championship,' says a Vatican official. 'Just as the whistle sounded for the half, a SOLIDARITY LIVES! banner went up on the screen and a tape came on calling for resistance.'"[1]

Furious communist officials in Warsaw and Moscow fumbled and fretted. None of their tactics or threats could arrest the avalanche for freedom. Most frustrating of all was the irresistible authority and influence of John Paul II from Rome inside his native Poland.

The movement that eventually toppled Euro-Communism had roots in 1978, when the Polish Cardinal Karol Wojtyla became Pope John Paul II. He quickly arranged a visit to his homeland. Crowds of a million voices cheered his rousing affirmations of life and liberty as fundamental gifts of God. In an unmistakable challenge to the atheistic government, John Paul appealed to the Pole's patriotism and religious heritage: "I beg you: ... Do not on your own cut yourself off from the roots from which we had our origins."

Poland could never be the same. After the pope flew back to Rome, his words stayed behind to inspire the birth of the Solidarity labor union. When the government condemned this direct threat to authoritarian rule, the pope invited Solidarity leader Lech Walesa to the Vatican. There he explicitly and emphatically endorsed his bold adventure in freedom.

That might have been too much for the pope's atheist enemies. Not long afterward came the assassination attempt upon the life of John Paul. A trail of evidence linked the gunman, a Muslim young man, to Eastern European communists. While blame for the shooting was never proven beyond question, certainly the motivation was there. It would make sense to silence the man most capable of shaking the foundations of international Communism.

But the attempt upon the pope's life failed. John Paul recovered and resumed his warfare against atheistic communism, finding a powerful ally in President Ronald Reagan. The cumulative effect of their combined efforts was just too much. "Step by reluctant step, the Soviets and the communist government of Poland bowed to the moral, economic and political pressure imposed by the Pope and the President. Jails were emptied, ... the Polish communist party turned fratricidal, and the country's economy collapsed in a haze of strikes and demonstrations and sanctions." The incredible climactic event was the election of Solidarity's Lech Walesa as the new Polish president.

Breaking forth from Poland, the wildfire of freedom spread throughout the Soviet block. The Berlin Wall did come down. As a shocked world watched, thousands of East Germans surged through the Brandenburg Gate. Stunned border guards, programmed to shoot, could only wave them through. West Berliners with open arms welcomed their unexpected visitors. Strangers joined in warm embrace, mingling their tears. Loved ones long separated found themselves together again.

Together again! Incredible but true–the Berlin Wall was no more. Joyful Germans danced in the streets. And the fall of the Wall was only the beginning. Almost overnight, freedom became an irresistible force throughout Eastern Europe. One by one the nations of Eastern Europe shook off the shackles of communism. Czechoslovakia, Hungary, Bulgaria–finally even Romania. Nobody, not even the most optimistic observer of world affairs, had expected so much so soon.

Finally the Soviet Union itself collapsed, and with it, seven decades of Euro-Communism. Ex-Soviet leader Gorbachev issued a public statement that the collapse of communism would have been impossible without the pope. Shortly before the end, Gorbachev had met with John Paul and proclaimed him to be the moral leader of this planet.

"This is the Holy Father," he announced to his wife, adding solemnly: "We are dealing with the highest religious authority of the world." The victorious pontiff responded, "I'm sure Providence prepared the way for this meeting."

## RENEWING THE HOLY ROMAN EMPIRE

Was that true? Was the providence of God at work fulfilling Bible prophecy in the incredible victory of the Western Christian alliance against the forces of atheism? Who could deny it? And now a new world order is emerging, bearing striking resemblance to the old Holy Roman Empire.

A recent op-ed piece in the New York Times observed: "When the East-West division of Europe was erased in 1989 with the collapse of the Berlin Wall, a new division immediately began forming: that between Central Europe and the Balkans."[2] A decade later, "the admission of Poland, the Czech Republic and Hungary into the North Atlantic Treaty Organization has formalized this dangerous historical and religious redivision of Europe: between a Roman Catholic and Protestant West and an Orthodox Christian and Muslim East."[3]

Atlantic Monthly noted: "By consummating this expansion, NATO has re-created a variation on the Holy Roman Empire, and also the borders dividing the Hapsburg and Ottoman Empires–true civilizational divides."[4] On March 12, 1999, documents were signed by Western leaders at the Harry S. Truman Library in Independence, Missouri. Students of Bible prophecy largely overlooked this historic event, perhaps because not many prophetic fulfillments of global significance happen in Missouri! Yet many secular commentators and European politicians did note the import of the event.

So did Russia, which vehemently objected to the expansion of NATO. In a few pages we'll see the prophetic significance of Russia's resistance to the reconstitution of NATO's new Holy Roman Empire and also Russia's alliance with militant Islam. But first let's get some perspective from a brief tour through history of the church's political adventures.

## HISTORY OF THE HOLY ROMAN EMPIRE

We begin now in sixth century Rome, with the emperor headquartered in Constantinople and the pope in charge of Rome. When barbarian armies attacked from the north, the church emerged from the crisis stronger than before, having Christianized the invaders. The three tribes that resisted suffered defeat from Roman armies, and the church began its 1260 year religio-political dynasty.

Meanwhile, however, a deadly threat was growing in the east. A powerful new religion was blossoming in the Arabian desert–Islam. Its founder, Muhammad, was born late in the sixth century in the city of Mecca, an important trading center. In his twenties he worked for a rich widow, whom he married. About the age of forty, Muhammad had a vision in which he believed God called him to present a special message to the world. Upon his death in 632, Muslim armies embarked on a quest for territory unlike anything the world had seen since Alexander the Great. They stormed through the Middle East and to the west across North Africa.

One Muslim naval attack involved as many as eighteen hundred ships. Outnumbered Christian defenders counterattacked with a terrifying secret weapon known as Greek fire, which burned more ferociously in water than on land. The exact formula of Greek fire remains unknown to this day. It wrought terrible havoc, causing the Islamic invaders to retreat. Constantinople remained under Christian control for the next seven hundred years.

Nevertheless, Islam continued its desert wildfire, burning up half of Christendom. Thousands became Muslims almost overnight. Jerusalem fell to Islamic rule, along with the entire Holy Land. Pilgrimages from Rome to Palestine became impossible.

Muslim armies even invaded Europe, gaining a foothold in the Swiss Alps. They swept across North Africa, crossing the Gibraltar to Spain and on into France. After intense fighting they met defeat from the army of Charles Martel at the Battle of Tours in 732. It was one of history's most important battles. For the moment, Europe was safe from Islam.

Seeking to guard against future Islamic incursions, Christian church and state strengthened their alliance and in the year 800 officially formed the Holy Roman Empire. Charlemagne was crowned its first ruler. The first task was to stabilize the loss of territory to Islam. Then the Holy Roman Empire went on the offensive by launching a series of Crusades, or church-sponsored military expeditions. In 1095 Pope Urban II rallied an army to win back the Holy Land.

In that First Crusade, armies of the church regained Jerusalem on July 15, 1099. It was a savage battle. Christian invaders plunged swords into every Muslim they found within the city. Blood flowed in the streets. Jews they slaughtered too, all in the name of Jesus, Prince of Peace.

And all in vain, too. Before long Muslims armies recaptured Jerusalem. Undeterred, the church sponsored additional expeditions, including the infamous Children's Crusade. Summer camp it wasn't. Recruited by the church and led by twelve-year-old Nicholas, they were Christian soldiers marching as to war. The enthusiastic but pathetically ill-prepared group departed Europe, planning to cross the Mediterranean Sea on dry land and recapture the tomb of Christ in Jerusalem. The kids never made it into combat with Muslims. Thousands died from disease along the way or were sold as slaves.

Meanwhile, Christianity was convulsed with internal strife. The church in Constantinople became weary of the Roman pope's authoritarianism and various other doctrinal disputes. One difference was that the Eastern Orthodox, with their emphasis on mysticism, were less aggressive than the Roman brand of Christianity. So in 1054, Eastern Christianity separated from Rome in what historians call the "Great Schism."

Today, nearly a millennium later, they remain separate. Under the Eastern Orthodox umbrella are fifteen different divisions, such as the Russian, Serbian, and Romanian national churches, chief among them being the Greek Orthodox Church. Although they all share with Rome a common revulsion for Islam, the major combatant against Muslims throughout the centuries was Rome.

In the heyday of the Holy Roman Empire, any person, group or nation that refused to submit to the pontiff's authority was marked for death. Not only Muslims and Jews, but fellow Christians fell victim to the Crusades. First the Orthodox, later the Protestants. The infamous Inquisitions then perfected the art of persecution.

Church leaders in Rome waged a multi-level assault upon the Protestant Reformation. At the Council of Trent they reorganized doctrines and practices, purging the worst abuses such as selling indulgences but reaffirming their core beliefs. Whenever spiritual persuasion failed to win back sheep that strayed from the shepherd at Rome, the cruel Inquisitions attempted to coerce their return.

When all else failed, Rome's strategy called for full-scale warfare against Protestant territories. But just as the armies of the Holy Roman Empire prepared to crush the Reformation in northern Europe, trouble stirred up to the south. Militant Muslims were on the march again. With Rome's resources diverted to that crisis, Protestants escaped destruction and continued growing. Some historians say that were it not for the Turk, there could not be a Protestant.

Protestants didn't appreciate militant Muslims any more than Catholics did. Christians everywhere during the Dark and Middle ages feared an Islamic invasion like people today dread a nuclear assault.

A century after Luther, war did break out between the Holy Roman Empire and Protestant princes, but too late to arrest the Reformation. The Thirty Years' War was the bloodiest in European history, up to that time. Ten million may have died. Finally relief came in 1648 with the Peace of Westphalia, probably the most important treaty of the millennium. It recognized the right of Protestant territories to exist without interference from Rome.

This was the first ray of dawn for modern religious tolerance. Rome was forced to concede the rights of private worship, liberty of conscience and emigration—only to those outside its control.

The Peace of Westphalia was the beginning of the end for the Holy Roman Empire. Final devastation came at the end of the eighteenth century through the French Revolution. This atheistic movement shook off the shackles of medieval religion, swerving like a drunkard toward the opposite extreme—total eradication of organized religion. Cathedrals were desecrated, priests were imprisoned. Then mobs broke into prisons and murdered the clergy. In Paris two centuries previously, the swords of church and state had swept through the streets murdering Protestants in the St. Bartholomew's Massacre. Now the persecutors became persecuted. The serene Seine River ran red with blood as priest and prince alike lost their heads to the greedy guillotine. The blade of that death machine rose and fell relentlessly, yet not quickly enough to satisfy those determined to wipe out anyone associated with the old relgio-political establishment. They demolished images of the virgin Mary, replacing them with the Goddess of Reason, a voluptuous woman of ill repute hailed by the blasphemous crowds as a symbol of their new freedom from the Christian God.

Meanwhile, the armies of France swarmed throughout Europe wiping out the last vestiges of the Holy Roman Empire. Napoleon's general Berthier stormed south into Rome in February of 1798 and attacked the Sistine Chapel, even as Pope Pius VI was conferring with his cardinals. French soldiers overcame the Swiss Guard, breaking down the doors with axes and and breaking up the meeting. They declared the pontiff's reign to be over. Then, ransacking the Vatican, they seized a fortune in gold, precious stones and art treasures before burning the vestments of the pope. They even ripped from the pope's finger the Ring of the Fisherman, symbol of authority at all papal coronations.

Stripped of all authority, the pope became a prisoner and died in foreign exile. It was the bitter ending of the Holy Roman Empire. Within a decade, the secular arm of the empire collapsed as the Austrian emperor capitulated.

Such was the rise and fall of the religious power that dominated Europe between 538 and 1798–exactly 1260 years, just as Bible prophecy had predicted more than 500 years before Christ.

## HAS THE CHURCH CHANGED?

Much has improved since medieval times. We must not blame the church of the present for the sins of its past. Protestants too have some skeletons in their closets of persecuted enemies–even in American colonial history. (We'll see the significance of this in chapter eight of this book.)

If Catholicism has changed now, it's only fair that we reassess our attitude toward Rome. So let's take a look at the church of today. What do we see?

There's a lot of love going on. The spirit of Mother Teresa lives on all over the world in Catholic hospitals, hospices, schools, orphanages, and soup kitchens.

But love is more than the ministry of compassion. Love also must be tough, as John Paul II personifies. Upon becoming pope, he immediately filled a void in moral leadership. In his first papal visit to the United States, he arrived in the rain at Boston's airport and announced: "To all I have come with a message of hope and peace—the hope and peace of Jesus Christ." That evening he pulled no punches in Boston Commons, exhorting the youth: "Faced with problems and disappointments," he said, many "escape from their responsibility, escape in selfishness, escape in sexual pleasure, escape in drugs, escape in violence, escape in indifference and cynical attitudes. But today I propose to you the option of love, which is the opposite of escape."

Tough love! John Paul continued: "Real love is demanding. I would fail in my mission if I did not tell you so. For it was Jesus—our Lord Jesus Himself—who said: 'You are my friends if you do what I command you.'"

Many thought teenagers might reject the pope's call to spiritual law and order. But no, nineteen thousand teenagers at Madison Square Garden the next day clapped and cheered as he urged them to discipline their lives. Lacking purpose in life, they welcomed the challenging morality of Pope John Paul. So did their parents, the survivors of the turbulent '60s.

Back then, the Roman Catholic Church itself swirled with change. In 1964 church leaders let in some fresh air with Vatican II. At that historic church council, Pope John XXIII prayed for a revival to renew the church and build a bridge to fellow Christians. Some remarkable and dramatic reforms followed. Among the most dramatic was the call for lay members to read God's Word. Also, worship is now in the language of the people rather than ancient Latin.

Since Vatican II, Catholics are reading their Bibles. The crucial question is: Has church doctrine changed to synchronize with Scripture?

Actually, the same basic doctrines established at the Council of Trent are still enforced today. All of them. Catholics continue to invoke the intercession of saints and use images in worship, in violation of the second commandment. Sunday still supplants the Sabbath, in violation of the fourth. Excitement for Marian miracles is multiplying. Purgatory remains as much an official doctrine of the church as ever, contradicting both the biblical truth about death and salvation as God's free gift.

Some Protestants are excited after dialoguing with Catholic scholars, imagining that they have reached a common understanding on the meaning of salvation by grace. But that word grace means profoundly different things to different people. Its basic New Testament meaning is revealed in the letters of the word itself: "GRACE = God's Riches At Christ's Expense." But when Catholics speak of grace they mean primarily the character virtues implanted by the Holy Spirit, which they always have regarded as meritorious—and the lack of which will plunge a person into purgatory.

Purgatory? Sorry, no grace there.

These are the same suffocating falsehoods that Rome taught in Luther's day. The Catholic concept of salvation remains entrenched since Trent. If that ever changes, proof will be the banishing of non-biblical and legalistic teachings such as purgatory and penance. And if Rome ever surrenders its tradition to Bible truth, it will keep all ten commandments as God gave them, not just eight.

Also there remains the notion of papal infallibility, the ultimate authority for enforcing celibacy upon priests and nuns. Yes, Scripture speaks of voluntary celibacy. The apostle Paul personally chose to be single, but most of his fellow apostles were married—even Peter (see 1 Corinthians 9:5). Thousands of priests and nuns have requested their right to follow St. Peter's example and get married, only to be turned down by his supposed successor in the Vatican. All who marry anyway are fired from church service, as if they had committed adultery.[5] Many Catholics wonder: Why does the pope speak so eloquently of religious liberty for society but refuse to grant freedom on a personal level?

Ultimately the issue isn't celibacy, it's spiritual authority. Does God want one man to have veto power over Scripture itself, controlling the lives of millions? Even if the pope is a good, sincere man? Something to think about carefully.

The Vatican worries that many Catholics, particularly in America, now reject church teachings and traditions not found in Scripture.

These enlightened Christians no longer accept non-biblical notions such as papal infallibility, enforced celibacy, purgatory, penance, prayer to saints, required confession to a priest and masses for the dead. Millions are delighted to discover the same Bible truths Luther did five hundred years ago. Perhaps without realizing it, they have become semi-Protestants. The pope knows this and is gravely concerned. To him, these disciples of Bible truth are apostates from true Catholicism.

So, to sum this up, methods have changed in the Roman Catholic Church but doctrine hasn't. Tradition still treads upon gospel truth. This leaves us with the sad conclusion that if Rome's core beliefs haven't reformed, neither has its status in Bible prophecy. Whatever it was in the days of Luther and the Council of Trent, it remains today.

## THE FUTURE OF UNITY

These days we hear much about Christian unity. It's a constant theme of Pope John Paul II, particularly in view of the new millennium. He intends to host a landmark Christian unity rally in Jerusalem during the year 2000. The concept is wonderful. Jesus prayed for unity–but also in that same prayer He said: "Sanctify them by Your truth. Your word is truth" (John 17:17). So true unity comes only when truth triumphs over tradition.

The Catholic concept of unity is quite different. Their leaders are ready and willing to dialogue, but they believe that Christian unity requires that sooner or later all believers must recognize the supreme authority of the pope as Christ's vicar on earth, His chief representative. Protestants and others need to understand this up front as they dialogue with Catholics, otherwise they are wasting their time and energy seeking a unity that can never happen on biblical terms.

Will the Christian world ever look to the pope for leadership? He is unquestionably the preeminent moral leader of the world. Western nations are growing weary of the secularism that, rooted in the French Revolution, has torn us away from our Christian heritage. The world has had its fling with Marxism, Darwinism, Freudism, secular feminism, and materialism.

Consider America. Once a God-fearing nation, we are essentially a post-Christian society in our behavior. Scandals in our government, shootings in our schools, slurping up stock market profits–we're getting sick of it all. The party's about over and soon we'll be ready to head for home.

Home to God. Home to spiritual roots. Sticking with our spouses. Raising our kids with proper values. Getting prayer back in schools. Posting the Ten Commandments in public places (ignoring the seventh-day Sabbath of the fourth commandment, of course). Having a weekly day set apart for family life, maybe Sunday.

Gallup polls report that our behavior lags behind our bedrock values. Like a bunch of school kids fooling around when they know they should be doing homework, we've engrossed ourselves with worldly distractions, though all along we've known better. There is a fundamental decency we know we need and down deep we really want. We are tired of politicians who lie to us. It's more than "the economy, stupid!" after all. We want trustworthy people leading our nation and teaching our kids.

Look past Hollywood, mired in immoral madness. Mainstream America has a burning yearning to get down to something deeper, back to something better than we've been doing with our lives. Despite the assault of secularism since the '60s, deep spiritual convictions remain. Even Western Europe with its near-empty cathedrals has Christianity in its subconscious. Everybody in England knew what to do when Princess Diana died–have a church service to memorialize her.

What would it take for NATO nations to reactivate their religious heritage and stir up spiritual zeal? A major international crisis that threatened our security. Imagine the effect of an Islamic terrorist bomb killing a thousand school children visiting Washington's Air and Space Museum. Or a blast at LAX blowing up an airline terminal. Or perhaps a United 777 coming from Paris exploding over the Atlantic. With all this happening and no end in sight, people would hasten back to God en masse.

When the prodigal West does come back to God, who will be waiting with the moral leadership nobody else is positioned to offer? Who else but the pope!

## TIME OF TROUBLE

The Bible does predict a last day alliance of militant Christianity, after the fashion of the Holy Roman Empire. Scripture also forecasts a revival of the historic rivalry between the West and its enemies to the east. Where? In that amazing book of Daniel we've been consulting throughout these pages.

Chapter 12 opens with a warning to earth's final generation: "At that time ... there will be a time of trouble, such as never was since there was a nation, even to that time" (Daniel 12:1). At what time? Go back a few verses and you'll notice in chapter 11 that this crisis is the climax of a colossal struggle between two great powers, labeled prophetically as the King of the North and the King of the South.

Long ago in Daniel's day the King of the North was Babylon. The Reformers recognized that in medieval times, Babylon represented the Holy Roman Empire. Today Babylon would represent the resurrection of that Holy Roman Empire with its confused mixture of tradition and truth. We'll see this from Scripture in upcoming pages.

Who then is the King of the South? In Daniel's time, Egypt. King Pharaoh there scorned the existence of God: "Who is the Lord, that I should obey His voice to let Israel go? I do not know the Lord" (Exodus 5:2). The modern counterpart would be those who likewise scorn the God we worship–basically Islamic forces allied with the remainder of the communist bloc. Muslims refuse to acknowledge the Lordship of Jesus Christ, regarding all believers as infidels. Militant Islamic governments suppress and outlaw Christian evangelism. They also present the greatest threat to the "new world order" that Western politicians have promoted.

Remember the warning in the New York Times that "the admission of Poland, the Czech Republic and Hungary into the North Atlantic Treaty Organization has formalized this dangerous historical and religious redivision of Europe: between a Roman Catholic and Protestant West and an Orthodox Christian and Muslim East."[6]

A dangerous situation indeed–an alliance of Catholics and Protestants under the banner of NATO in the West versus a coalition of Muslims and Orthodox linked with governments left over from the communist era.

NATO won its 1999 war against Serbia but in the process actually strengthened the King of the South alliance–the axis that bonds Russia, China, and fundamentalist Islamic nations. Witness the amazing outpouring of hostility against the nations of NATO because of the bombing of Serbia and the Chinese embassy. Immediately Moscow and Beijing held high level meetings to plot strategy against the West. Officials of both nations also consulted with their militant Islamic allies, whom they supply with nuclear warfare expertise and missiles to wield against the West and against Israel, America's most dependable friend in the Middle East. (If you noticed, militant Islamic nations expressed little concern for the ethnic Albanian Muslims NATO rescued in Kosovo. They hate America, the "Great Satan," much more than they support non-fundamentalist Muslims at war with their friend, Serbia. Iraq even helped Serbia build bomb shelters to protect them as they implemented the ethnic cleansing of Kosovo.)

So the stage is set for an Armageddon-style religio-political showdown between the King of the North and the King of the South. How far will we go with this retro medieval-type union of religion and politics? Will we trade religious liberty for national security to escape a military or economic crisis? Will persecution arise again?

## GOOD NEWS AND BAD NEWS

We had better be alert while awaiting the coming of Christ. Then we can rejoice that God, even while warning of the big time of trouble ahead, promises: "And at that time your people shall be delivered, every one who is found written in the book" (Daniel 12:1). This is heaven's book of life, in which our names are recorded when we accept the gospel–God's good news about salvation through the life, death and resurrection of Jesus Christ. He will deliver every one of His committed people, bringing us safely to heaven when Jesus comes:

"After these things I looked, and behold, a great multitude which no one could number, of all nations, tribes, peoples, and tongues, standing before the throne and before the Lamb, clothed with white robes, with palm branches in their hands, and crying out with a loud voice, saying, 'Salvation belongs to our God who sits on the throne, and to the Lamb!' ... Then one of the elders answered, saying to me, 'Who are these arrayed in white robes, and where did they come from?' And I said to him, ... 'These are the ones who come out of the great tribulation, and washed their robes and made them white in the blood of the Lamb'" (Revelation 7:9-14).

How thrilling that will be! Picture yourself praising God with the saints of all the ages, waving palm branches of victory in Jesus.

Do you want to belong to God's triumphant heavenly family? Your reaction this moment to His invitation is determining your eternal destiny.

---

[1] Carl Bernstein, "The Holy Alliance," *Time*, (February 1992): electronic edition.

[2] Robert D. Kaplan, "After the Ottoman Empire," *New York Times* (January 17, 1999), electronic edition.

[3] *Ibid.*

[4] Robert D. Kaplan, "The Fulcrum of Europe," *Atlantic Monthly* (September 1998), electronic edition.

[5] As of this writing, one former Episcopalian priest in the United States who joined the Roman Catholic Church while already married is being approved for the Catholic priesthood while still keeping his wife. The traditional restrictive policy regarding celibacy remains unchanged toward Catholics who already are priests or who wish to qualify for priesthood.

[6] Kaplan, *New York Times.*

# Chapter seven
## A GRAVE NEW WORLD

So you're watching the Yankees game when suddenly the station breaks away to the newsroom.

You're not thrilled about the intrusion. Bases loaded, tying run on second. How dare they interrupt my game! Good grief, it's the playoffs!

Then you notice the somber-faced newscaster with tousled hair announcing:

"A tragedy has struck our nation's capitol this evening. At Union Station near the Capitol Building, a pressurized canister containing poison gas was set off on the Red Line subway platform during rush hour, spewing noxious fumes. Scores of passengers are being taken to area hospitals. Dozens are feared already dead.

"Authorities are uncertain what type of poison gas is involved, though cyanide is suspected. Unconfirmed reports are that one minute before the attack, a young man, perhaps of Middle Eastern descent, activated a timer connected to a spraying device. He then ran out of the station northbound on North Capital Street and remains at large.

"Police have sealed off the area. Rescue workers and FBI agents equipped with gas masks are swarming the site. We'll keep you updated throughout the evening as details of this tragedy become available."

Wow. This is bigger than a ball game. What a calamity!

But the evening is still young. People have hardly yet begun to die.

In Manhattan's Broadway theater district, tuxedo-clad customers are running out of restaurants and writhing on sidewalks, vomiting violently. Rumors are that the water supply is poisoned. Speaking of water, the George Washington Bridge collapses into the Hudson River after a massive fiery explosion lights the night sky.

What a night! What's next?

Terrible beyond imagination but not beyond belief. Jesus warned of devastating pestilence in various places (Matthew 24:7). So have secular experts with inside information on terrorism. Notice this recent Washington Post opinion piece by the U. S. Secretary of Defense: "Preparing for a Grave New World."

"At least twenty-five countries, including Iraq and North Korea, now have—or are in the process of acquiring and developing—weapons of mass destruction." These arsenals include chemical toxins and biotoxins, such as smallpox, "the horrific infectious virus that decimated entire nations down the ages and against which the global population is currently defenseless."

Secretary Cohen continues: "Also looming is the chance that these terror weapons will find their way into the hands of individuals and independent groups—fanatical terrorists and religious zealots. ... This is not hyperbole. It is reality."

He recalls that those who bombed the World Trade Center in 1993 were also stockpiling toxins that could have killed thousands. In the aftermath of such attacks, "hospitals would become warehouses for the dead and the dying. A plague more monstrous than anything we have experienced could spread with all the irrevocability of ink on tissue paper. Ancient scourges would quickly become modern nightmares."

And then he soberly summarizes: "Welcome to the grave New World of terrorism."

Wow. What a warning from an ultimate insider! We can only wonder what else government leaders know that they don't tell us so as not to cause chaos.

Imagine a terrorist event in your locality. Picture the panic as sirens wail without ceasing. Banks and other businesses are abandoned, except for looters scurrying through shattered storefronts lugging jugs of water. National Guard tanks rumble through smoky streets, shoving aside wrecked taxis and police cars. Camouflage green bulldozers dig mass graves for countless anonymous body bags. Loudspeakers blare orders from the Emergency Broadcast System—only this time it's not just a test.

A grave new world indeed. Nobody cares now about gossiping at Starbucks or Sammy Sosa home runs or what's happening with Dow Jones. If he were around, he might be inside a body bag by now, anyway.

From peace to panic in one short day. We're at war, but we don't know where the enemy is or how to stop him. It's a similar scenario to the recent movie The Siege, but without the irrationally happy ending. Reality is more like a Tom Clancy novel, only this time you can't put the book down and take a break when the action gets too intense.

## END TIME ANTICHRIST

Who's behind all this? It's probably too big for a domestic militia squad to pull off. Maybe some mysterious millennial doomsday cult inflicting the ultimate millennimania. Most people suspect Islamic terrorists, even though scattered voices in the media warn against rushing to judgment. But it's hard to ignore all that dancing in the streets of Damascus and Baghdad, with American flags burning. Yes, most Muslims are gentle, generous, peaceable people, but there is that radical minority committed to carnage. For two decades militant mullahs have sent students surging through the streets of Tehran and Tripoli shouting "Death to America!" Perhaps it's time we took radical Muslims at their word. After all, thousands of them graduated from terrorist training schools dedicating their lives to causing such crises.

Is this all leading us to Armageddon, that last great battle? Will the antichrist be involved? What does the Bible say?

Our last chapter noted the end time alliance of powerful forces resisting Western Christianity, symbolized in Scripture as the King of the South. This is the modern counterpart to the medieval Turks, who opposed the Holy Roman Empire. These days the anti-western axis includes the various representatives of militant Islam, Russia and other former communist powers hostile to the West (many of which are linked to Orthodox Christianity). And let's not forget to include that muscle-flexing giant of the Far East, communist China. Some of these powers have nuclear capabilities, with several others getting close. Most are well-equipped with conventional weapons, plus those of mass destruction such as germ and chemical stockpiles.

Some would nominate this King of the South alliance as the antichrist. Well, certainly there is fierce opposition to Christ, at least as He is presented in Scripture. But remember that the Bible warns against deception in association with the antichrist. "Let no one deceive you by any means" (2 Thessalonians 2:3). Deception so difficult to discern, Jesus said, that it would threaten to trick even His elect, the saints (see Matthew 24:24). Now, would a committed believer be deceived if an Islamic or atheistic power tried to close down our churches and abolish the worship of Jesus Christ? That would be persecution, yes. But no believer would be deceived by outright opposition to the name of Jesus. So the King of the South, although a persecuting power, cannot be the end-time antichrist.

How about the King of the North? We saw how the Reformers concluded from Scripture that the medieval church with its Holy Roman Empire served that role in their time. And the same basic fallacies that corrupted Western Christianity through the centuries are still taught today. At the dawn of the new millennium, this King of the North power, otherwise known as spiritual Babylon, continues to cause confusion by upholding traditions invented by human leaders rather than accepting the sole authority of God in Scripture. It claims to uphold the gospel of God's grace while undermining the essence of Christian faith. It exalts the adoration of saints, despite the second commandment. It applauds God's law while breaking the seventh-day Sabbath of the fourth commandment.

All that amounts to deception. Big time. Even while standing firm against the immorality and materialism of Western society, the church still dishonors God's law and grace in some of its fundamental teachings. Remember, Muslims also condemn the same sins of the West, for which they label us the Great Satan. Does that earn them God's endorsement, just because they promote moral values? Not as long as they resist the full truth of God's grace and His law through Jesus Christ. The same would go for the church of Rome or any other church. Are we being urged to scout the horizon for some future Antichrist power, when all the time it has been flourishing in our own neighborhood?

Along with the deceptions, the Bible warns about misleading miracles associated with this antichrist power that arose early within Christian history, operated throughout the centuries, and then will have a final fatal role at the end of time:

"And then the lawless one will be revealed, whom the Lord will consume with the breath of His mouth and destroy with the brightness of His coming. The coming of the lawless one is according to the working of Satan, with all power, signs, and lying wonders, and with all unrighteous deception among those who perish, because they did not receive the love of the truth, that they might be saved" (2 Thessalonians 2:8-10).

Here we see that the antichrist power will work all kinds of miracles and lying wonders until finally meeting destruction at the second coming of Jesus. Could this possibly involve a miraculous false appearance of Mary, mother of Jesus? Even Christ Himself? Would a counterfeit Jesus be the ultimate deception of the antichrist power? Perhaps in association with a staged return to Jerusalem? Would this have any connection with the battle of Armageddon?

## A PLACE CALLED ARMAGEDDON

Just once does our Bible mention the word Armageddon, in the book of Revelation:

"For they are the spirits of demons, performing signs, which go out to the kings of the earth and of the whole world, to gather them to the battle of that great day of God Almighty.... And they gathered them together to the place called in Hebrew, Armageddon" (Revelation 16:14,16).

This "battle of that great day of God Almighty" is earth's final conflict. More than human forces will participate–the spiritual armies of God and Satan will clash (see Revelation 17:14). Armageddon climaxes the great controversy between good and evil.

Where will this battle be fought? History offers no record of any place called Armageddon, but Scripture offers some hints. Our text says the word Armageddon comes from the Hebrew. In that language, the word combines har, meaning "mountain," and mageddon, which appears to link with "Megiddo." So the name Armageddon can be understood as "mountain of Megiddo."

The mountain of Megiddo–this gives us something to work with. Thousands of years ago, Megiddo was a small but significant fortress city north of Jerusalem near the plain of Esdraelon. Once the Bible calls this plain itself the plain of Megiddo. This might seem to provide a logical battlefield, but then we recall that Armageddon involves not a plain but a mountain.

So where is this mountain of Megiddo? A mountain with spiritual significance for the armies of heaven.

Going to the location of ancient Megiddo could help us analyze Armageddon. Eastward from the Mediterranean port city of Haifa, we follow the Carmel ridge. After passing the northeastern ridge of Carmel we arrive at the ruins of the ancient city. Towering over the landscape at Megiddo is Mount Carmel.

Perhaps Mount Carmel is our solution. Does it symbolize Mount Megiddo, the scene of Armageddon? What may have happened at Mount Carmel that would shed light on Armageddon?

One unforgettable day Carmel hosted a showdown between God and His enemies. Elijah the prophet called the nation to come to the mountain. He challenged them to decide between true and false worship. Hear his heart-gripping appeal:

"How long will you falter between two opinions? If the Lord is God, follow Him; but if Baal, then follow him" (1 Kings 18:21).

God won a tremendous victory that day at Carmel. Israel repented and reaffirmed their commitment to Him rather than to the pagan sun god. Unitedly they declared: "The Lord, He is God! The Lord, He is God" (1 Kings 18:39). After taking their stand for God and His government, they executed the leaders who had deceived them.

We see then that the summons to Mount Carmel involved judgment—evaluating God and His government. And then a judgment of all who rebelled against Him. Should we expect a similar type of judgment associated with Armageddon? What does Scripture say?

The Bible teaches that Armageddon will come during the seven plagues at the end of earth's history. Let's discover something about these plagues. The Lord has been patient all these years, sending sunshine and rain even upon His enemies. Suddenly now He sends wrath instead of rain. Why?

Has some type of judgment taken place in heaven? Has a verdict been reached? Revelation 11 tells us:

"Then the seventh angel sounded: And there were loud voices in heaven, saying, 'The kingdoms of this world have become the kingdoms of our Lord and of His Christ, and He shall reign forever and ever!' And the twenty-four elders who sat before God on their thrones fell on their faces and worshiped God, saying: 'We give You thanks, O Lord God Almighty, the One who is and who was and who is to come, because You have taken Your great power and reigned. The nations were angry, and Your wrath has come, and the time of the dead, that they should be judged, and that You should reward Your servants the prophets and the saints, and those who fear Your name, small and great, and should destroy those who destroy the earth'" (Revelation 11:15-18).

An amazing scenario. What's happening here? A time to be judged, the text tells us. A judgment up in heaven while life continues here on earth–just like at Carmel, God's government must be vindicated before He assumes His authority to punish the wicked.

What's the background behind this judgment? Way back when Satan was banished from heaven to this earth, he claimed the right to represent our world in the councils of heaven. (You can read the story in the first two chapters of the Old Testament book of Job.) God defended His government before the heavenly host against His enemy's challenge.

All heaven watched as Satan afflicted Job with all sorts of trouble, trying to discourage him from trusting in God. But Job remained faithful–just as God's people will in the last days. Job's trust and loyalty vindicated God against the charges of the devil.

What's the purpose of this judgment? Realizing that loyalty depends upon the ability to trust, God cares about His reputation. So He determines to prove Himself trustworthy, allowing Himself to be audited.

This same type of judgment occurs in the business world today. A corporation president, charged with dishonesty, may decide to open the books so every employee can see he has been just and fair. He wants to be trusted. If he hasn't been honest in his dealings, then he will do everything possible to prevent such an audit.

God has nothing to hide, so He invites inspection of His government. The apostle Paul understood this judgment when he wrote, "Let God be found true, though every man be found a liar, as it is written. 'That Thou mightest be justified in Thy words, and mightest prevail when Thou art judged'" (Romans 3:4 / NASB).

So God will prevail when He is judged. Just as He prevailed in the days of Job. Just as He won His case at Mount Carmel. God convinces His creation He is worthy of their worship. Satan's challenge is defeated at Armageddon. The kingdoms of the world become God's beyond dispute. Citizens of the universe stand behind Him as He rewards His people and punishes rebellion with the seven last plagues.

Is this judgment portrayed in the book of Revelation? Come with me to chapter 5. In Revelation 4 and 5, the apostle John describes what many consider to be the actual judgment scene in heaven's temple. Angels–millions of them, gather to weigh the evidence, the evidence about God and His followers on earth. Scrolls, old fashioned books, are opened. (By the way, in Scripture the opening of books indicates judgment. See Daniel 7:10.)

## HE ALONE IS WORTHY

What's happening in the courts of heaven? Let's listen in:

"Then I saw a strong angel proclaiming with a loud voice: 'Who is worthy to open the scroll and to loose its seals?' And no one in heaven or on the earth or under the earth was able to open the scroll, or to look at it" (Revelation 5:2-3).

Who is worthy? That's the vital question. With agonized interest, John waits to see who will pass the judgment.

But nobody is worthy. "No one in heaven," not even the patriarch Enoch, who walked with God and was taken up to heaven without seeing death. "Nobody on the earth"–currently alive on earth–measures up to the scrutiny of judgment. Not even John himself, a disciple of Jesus. And nobody "under the earth"–nobody in the grave–is worthy.

So John begins to "weep greatly." Disappointed curiosity? No, much more. He's worried about the judgment. If nobody can survive the scrutiny of heaven's court, what hope does he have?

Everyone is unworthy. Everyone, that is, but Jesus: "But one of the elders said to me, "Do not weep. Behold, the Lion of the tribe of Judah, the Root of David, has prevailed to open the scroll and to loose its seven seals" (verse 5).

What comfort for our hearts–the Lord Jesus Christ is declared worthy! He prevails in heaven's court. And when our Savior wins the verdict, we win too, for our lives belong to Him. We overcome in the blood of the Lamb!

Remember the story of those plagues in Egypt? What saved God's people from the death angel? Blood on their doorposts. God promised, "When I see the blood, I will pass over you; and the plague shall not be on you to destroy you when I strike the land of Egypt" (Exodus 12:13).

The blood–that's what counts! The blood of Jesus. In our Savior's blood, we're safe from the plagues.

When every soul decides for life or death, earth's harvest will be ripe. All who trust in Jesus are sealed for eternal life. And those who refuse God's salvation will lose their lives.

Remember the volcano eruption at Mount St. Helens? Then you may have heard about Harry Truman. Not the former president. This particular Harry Truman owned the Mount St. Helens Lodge in Washington state. With his neighbors, Harry had been warned about an imminent eruption. But some, including 84-year-old Harry, refused all attempts to save them from their beloved mountain.

Harry boasted to his would-be rescuers, "There's nothing that mountain could do to scare me off." St. Helens, evidently, was like a friend to him. He felt safe, having lived there 54 years. He even bragged: "No one knows more about this mountain than Harry, and it don't dare blow up on him."

But it did. On the morning of May 18, 1980, an explosion 2,500 times more powerful than the blast that ripped Hiroshima burst upon Harry as an overwhelming surprise. Today he and dozens of others lie buried beneath the volcanic mud. They risked their lives and lost.

The warning came, but they resisted being saved. Somehow human nature doesn't like warnings.

In the book of Revelation, just before the destruction of this world, God sends three angels with special worldwide warnings. Each angel proclaims one part of God's final admonition to the human race.

These angels, of course, are symbolic of their messages. They don't fly overhead with loudspeakers. Here is the first warning:

"Then I saw another angel flying in the midst of heaven, having the everlasting gospel to preach to those who dwell on the earth–to every nation, tribe, tongue, and people–saying with a loud voice,

'Fear God and give glory to Him, for the hour of His judgment has come; and worship Him who made heaven and earth, the sea and springs of water'" (Revelation 14:6,7).

Here's the everlasting gospel, the same wonderful message of salvation dear to Paul and Martin Luther. Now there's a new urgency, because "the hour of His judgment has come." A judgment like that at Mount Carmel long ago.

Next comes the second angel, warning about the false worship of Babylon—religious confusion. Then finally the third angel, sounding the alarm about the mark of the beast. (Next chapter we will look at this famous and intriguing mark.)

So it is that every soul decides for life or death. Those faithful to God receive His seal. The disobedient receive the mark of the beast and the plagues. After the seventh and last plague, Christ returns to airlift His people from Armageddon.

As the New International Commentary on the New Testament confirms:

"Har-Mageddon is symbolic of the final overthrow of all the forces of evil by the might and power of God. ... God will emerge victorious and take with him all who have placed their faith in him."[1]

So that's what Armageddon is all about—a showdown between truth or error, loyalty to God or to the powers of evil. While there certainly will be devastating battles among the armies of earth, the dominant theme of Scripture is that Armageddon centers around a spiritual conflict with fierce deceptions. These are the deceptions of the antichrist, associated with the King of the North.

## A COUNTERFEIT CHRIST

Ponder the following description of prophetic insight from Ellen G. White, written a century ago, of what a counterfeit appearance of Jesus might look like at the climax of Armageddon:

"Fearful sights of a supernatural character will soon be revealed in the heavens, in token of the power of miracle-working demons. ... As the crowning act in the great drama of deception, Satan himself will personate Christ. ... In different parts of the earth, Satan will manifest himself among men as a majestic being of dazzling brightness. ... The shout of triumph rings out upon the air: 'Christ has come! Christ has come!' The people prostrate themselves in adoration before him, while he lifts up his hands and pronounces a blessing upon them, as Christ blessed His disciples when He was upon the earth."[2]

Imagine the devil appearing in Jerusalem impersonating Christ, perhaps appearing with an apparition of Mary His mother. The imposter of our Savior would probably bless the children, heal the sick, and promote world peace through the total cessation of terrorism and renunciation of mass weapons of destruction. The message of unity and love would be backed by incredible miracles. Such a deception is almost irresistible.

Now we see how the King of the North will conquer the world. Not by a military might that overcomes terrorism but by uniting everyone behind these deceptive miracles. The text we saw spoke of the "spirits of demons, performing signs, which go out to the kings of the earth and of the whole world, to gather them to the battle of that great day of God Almighty" (Revelation 16:13-14).

Mark those words–the whole world will be gathered together, or united, through satanic miracles. Even the King of the South alliance, then, will ultimately cease its terrorism and convert to counterfeit Christianity. Then the world powers represented by the King of the North and the King of the South will unite to do battle–not against each other but against God's faithful remnant, whom we will talk about shortly.

Atheists from communist China and the former Soviet bloc, along with evolutionists in the West., will all receive undeniable and irresistible evidence of the supernatural and join the ranks of the deceived.

Consider Russia. Way back in 1917, the Fatima apparition predicted that this nation at last will be converted. Such will be the persuasive power of Marian apparitions and other miracles. Not only the atheists, but the Orthodox in their mystical appreciation for Mary would quickly join the Christian West in honoring the lady of Fatima.

What about Muslims? Many Muslims, though they may hate Christianity, expect Jesus to return as a prophet to Jerusalem. So they may welcome the appearance of a miraculous antichrist. As for honoring Mary, one intriguing detail about Fatima is that the founder of Islam, Mohammad, had a beloved daughter by that name. Muslims might see this as an indication from Allah that these apparitions are for them, too. The Koran even acknowledges that Mary is the highest woman in heaven. (Actually, the real Mary is not in heaven but is sleeping in the grave with all the rest of God's saints, awaiting the coming of Jesus to awaken them from death. See 1 Thessalonians 4:16-18 and 1 Corinthians 15:22-23, 51-55).

As for Jews, what effect will these apparitions of Jesus and Mary have upon them? The ABC telecast "Good Morning America Sunday" recently aired a fascinating segment: "The Cult of Mary." Here are excerpts from a Jewish author, Naomi Wolf, commenting on the Marian apparitions:

"I'm not Catholic. But as a Jewish girl looking at what moves people, I was really struck by how not just Catholics seem to be seeking out the Virgin Mary as a source of consolation, of help in times of trouble. ... And all over the world, Mary and apparitions are appearing in Rwanda and Sarajevo, to people who are Catholic and not Catholic, like an apparition in North Africa to a bunch of Muslims. ...

"I'm an observant Jew. And what strikes me as a non-Catholic is that when these apparitions [of Mary] appear to people, ... her message is a political message of peacemaking, of reconciliation. And what is amazing to me as a non-Catholic is that she's actually starting to say all religions are equally valid, all religions are a path to God. That's quite moving to me. ... And that means extending a hand across the divisions of race and across divisions of religion ... And it means being open to each other's spiritual traditions."[3]

What an amazing testimony to the power of these miraculous apparitions to influence even an observant Jew toward seeking unity and reconciliation through a shared experience in the miraculous.

How would India and the other homelands of Eastern religions react to the antichrist? They acknowledge many divine expressions of the "universal god force" and have no reason to reject these new apparitions. The same would hold true in the Southern Hemisphere for tribal Africa, native South Americans and people of Oceania. In America, Western Europe, Australia and New Zealand, New Age adherents already believe in the miraculous. As for Christians themselves all around the world, remember that Jesus said the deceptions before His coming would be so fierce that even true believers will be tested. Superficial saints will certainly be swept away with the satanic delusions.

So we can expect miraculous personages masquerading as Jesus and Mary to plead for unity and inspire commitment to reconciliation, disarmament, and world peace. "No more terrorism! No more weapons of mass destruction." Count on the enemy to counterfeit angels of God, prophets from Bible times, UFOs–anything and everything that might trick our tabloid generation. Convinced by the satanic super show of miracles, the whole world will ultimately convert to counterfeit worship.

## EVERYONE BUT THE REMNANT

Everyone, everywhere will be deceived! Everyone, that is, except Christ's true disciples, the "elect." He said: "My sheep hear My voice, and I know them, and they follow Me" "Yet they will by no means follow a stranger, but will flee from him" (John 10:27, 5).

Naturally, the devil is not happy about their persistent faithfulness and refusal to sway to his deceptions. And so "the dragon was wroth with the woman, and went to make war with the remnant of her seed, which keep the commandments of God, and have the testimony of Jesus Christ" (Revelation 12:17 / KJV).

Yes, God will have for Himself a remnant on this earth. With the final confederation of evil arrayed against them, they remain totally committed disciples of the real Christ. They choose to believe the Bible instead of their senses and would rather die than betray God's truth.

As the corrupt powers of earth unite against God's truth, the Good Shepherd is earnestly working to gather all His sheep away from falsehoods and deceptions and safely into His remnant fold: "And other sheep I have which are not of this fold; them also I must bring, and they will hear My voice; and there will be one flock and one shepherd" (John 10:16).

Do you want to belong to Christ's faithful remnant? You can pause and make that commitment to Him just now, before you turn the page. Then why not share the joy of your decision with a friend?

[1] *The Book of Revelation,* New International Commentary on the New Testament, (Grand Rapids, Mich.: Eerdmans Publishing Co., 1977), p. 302.

[2] Ellen G. White, *The Great Controversy,* (Boise, Id.: Pacific Press Publishing Association, 1911), p. 624.

[3] Naomi Wolf, interview, "The Cult of Mary," *Good Morning America Sunday* (February 7, 1999): electronic transcript, www.abcnews.com.

# Chapter eight
## DEATH ON A SUNDAY

It's halftime at the Super Bowl. Millions are watching America's biggest party. Inside the stadium, sixty thousand sports fans whistle and ogle as erotic dancers gyrate on stage amid a laser light extravaganza. A fireworks spectacular concludes the show, dazzling the crowd.

Suddenly a huge, blinding explosion, incredible in force, incinerates the stadium. Everyone dies instantly. A mushroom cloud forms overhead and hovers above the scene of horror.

As the news sends shockwaves through the nation, panic and pandemonium prevail. A nuclear attack within America! Who would do such a thing? Why? What will they do next?

Answers quickly come. A fax arrives at the London Times newsroom from somewhere in Lebanon. An obscure Islamic terrorist group is boasting about the bomb, giving all the glory to Allah.

So it is a religious attack. Panic turns to anger. White hot rage burns against Muslims everywhere. Innocent Arab taxi drivers waiting for customers at Washington's Dulles Airport are yanked out of their vehicles and shot.

The terrorists claiming responsibility for the attack declare a jihad, or holy war. It will continue until America, the "Great Satan" and source of the world's worst wickedness, submits to the will of Allah. Meaning what, specifically? For the terror to stop we must cease all support for Israel, withdraw American armed forces stationed in Muslim countries, and pay a bounty of 10 billion dollars for the pharmaceutical factory destroyed during that 1998 missile attack.

Naturally, America can't meet those demands. We are irrevocably bonded with Israel. And there's no way we can abandon our military presence in strategic areas like Kuwait. Ten billion dollars for that Sudanese factory? Forget about it. We'll never be held hostage like that, the president declares.

So the terror escalates. A bombing here, a poison outbreak there. Some of it high tech, some of it low tech. All of it chaos. The FBI is helpless to stop it. Every time they arrest the members of one jihad cell, others eagerly spring into action. Death to them means nothing as long as they can take a few Americans with them out of this world.

## A DIFFERENT KIND OF WAR

The United States becomes a cultural and economic wasteland. Museums and schools are shut. So is the New York Stock Exchange after a bomb threat on Wall Street. Stores are barricaded. Mobs forage for bread and milk. The World Series is canceled–nobody would come and risk getting nuked. America is no longer land of the free and home of the brave.

Overseas, London is bombed daily, just as it was in 1940. Brussels, Bonn, Milan, all of them are under attack. Paris too. And, of course, Jerusalem. Oh, Jerusalem!

The entire Christian West is held hostage by shadowy religious fanatics. We're terrified of those wiry young men with fierce dark eyes and white skullcaps. Thanks to them, prosperity is past. The party's over. This is war.

Actually, war already began several years ago when Osama Bin Laden, widely regarded as the world's most notorious terrorist leader, announced a jihad (Islamic holy war) against the United States. He then masterminded and executed the deadly bombings on U.S. embassies in Africa and sponsored other terrorist events. America struck back with a massive cruise missile attack on his headquarters in Afghanistan. Ben Laden survived and seems more determined than ever to devastate the United States. Ominous reports indicate that his organization has stockpiled both chemical and biological weapons of mass destruction and is even accumulating nuclear capability.

Combating domestic terrorism is a drastically different type of warfare than America is accustomed to. The World Trade Center bombing and aborted plot to blow up the United Nations and the Lincoln Tunnel marked the beginning of a new era of danger for the United States. For first time since the War of 1812, the mainland of the United States is threatened with a foreign invasion. It's one thing to fight a war in Europe or Vietnam; it's another thing to do battle in our own cities.

Something else new is that the enemy isn't an army. There are no front lines behind which you can take shelter. And for the first time,

U.S. civilians are specifically targeted. Terrorist leader Bin Laden declares that he makes no difference between the military or civilians, men or women. He wants to harm or destroy us all.

What's more, America for the first time is engaged in a holy war. Just like the old Crusades, only this time the Christian West is the victim.

The president declares a state of national emergency. Politicians and preachers flood the airwaves urging–demanding–that America get back to God. There is a general sense that He is punishing America for "wreckreation" such as Natural Born Killers and violent video games, homosexuality, and tolerating the kind of leadership that kept Kenneth Starr busy.

America has sinned! Our only hope is from above, lest we perish. It's a spiritual problem. So we need a spiritual solution.

The president announces a national day of prayer. Congress immediately affirms it. Previously feuding Republicans and Democrats congregate on the steps of the Capitol Building to beg God to keep His promise: "If My people who are called by My name will humble themselves, and pray and seek My face, and turn from their wicked ways, then I will hear from heaven, and will forgive their sin and heal their land" (2 Chronicles 7:14).

Despite fear of public places, a million supplicants crowd the Washington Mall to pray. People prostrate themselves face first on the grass and gravel, imploring God to rescue America. Posters rebuke everything from beer to bikinis. Anyone who fails to join the mass prayer crusade is labeled an atheistic nonconformist.

The national day of prayer comes and goes, but the terror continues. Within a week, a major Texas oil refinery blows up. Dozens die and gasoline becomes rationed. A marine helicopter over the American Embassy in Saudi Arabia is hit by a shoulder-fired missile. More dead. Then a smallpox epidemic breaks out in Boston. Since that old killer had been conquered, we stopped immunizing against it. But now thousands fall prey to an awful ancient death.

The president goes on TV from the Oval Office. On his desk there's a crucifix never seen there before as he solemnly announces that he is invoking his emergency powers. Instantly democracy becomes a dictatorship. The purpose is simple survival, he explains. Few mind their loss of liberty in hopes of restoring national security.

When will it all end? How will it end?

## WAITING ALL THE TIME

At crucial times throughout U. S. history, presidents have activated their little known but extremely powerful emergency provisions. These powers are there and ready to be enforced.

In the 19th century, for example, no less than the great emancipator himself, Abraham Lincoln, implemented these presidential war powers during the superheated hostilities of the Civil War. Lincoln, who exercised his war powers to proclaim the freedom of slaves, ironically used that same authority to impair the civil rights of others for the sake of national security. Lincoln regarded spying, sabotage, recruiting for the enemy, and other threats so grave that he resorted to military arrests of civilians and the suspension of rights to a fair trial and appeals process.

Badgered by scattered criticism, Lincoln explained: "I felt that measures otherwise unconstitutional might become lawful by becoming indispensable to the preservation of the Constitution through the preservation of the nation."[1] And so America's patron saint of freedom became something of a dictator.

In the past century, such a triumph of executive war powers over the Bill of Rights became legal in 1917 when the United States plunged into World War I. That June, the Wilson administration prodded Congress to pass the Lever Food Control Bill, which authorized the government to mobilize against food shortages and escalating prices. The bill was so broad as to subjugate virtually the entire national economy under any regulation the president considered necessary to vanquish the Germans.

When Hitler's rising sun launched another war followed by Japan's blitzkrieg on Pearl Harbor, Roosevelt expanded further the emergency powers of his presidency. Congress and the courts complied.[2]

One of the darkest chapters in the history of the Supreme Court was leaving unchecked Roosevelt's imprisonment of more than one hundred thousand Japanese Americans, seventy percent of whom were U.S. citizens. Arresting them at their homes and jobs, the government shipped them to detention camps for up to four years of imprisonment. Amazingly, "no more than twelve openly resisted, and four of these cases eventually reached the U.S. Supreme Court."[3]

Public opinion and the media let it happen, while the Supreme Court sustained the government's detention policies.

Evidently you can't count on the court in a national emergency. You can't count on the Congress, the president, the media, your local police. Even your best friends can't save you. You can only count on God.

And so, during our proposed terrorist scenario of the new millennium, America is praying up a storm. Panic prevails and rage deepens. Anyone so unfortunate as to look Arabic is subject to arrest, impromptu beatings, even lynching. In this "grave New World of terrorism," Muslims–or members of any minority religion–are under instant suspicion. Unofficially but unmistakably, we declare our own holy war against the radical Islamic world that has shattered our world.

## HOLY WARS OF HISTORY

Going back to the days of the Holy Roman Empire, the Christian West has a rich heritage of holy wars, forcing its faith upon Muslims and other nonconformists. The roots of such intolerance for "heretics" began growing in the early fourth century, when the pagan Constantine announced his conversion to Christ. Not content to merely share his faith, he ordered Roman soldiers to be baptized. How? He just marched them all into the sea.

Soon Constantine began legislating religion in general society. In the year 321, he declared Sunday the national day of worship. Six decades later Christianity became the official state religion by order of Emperor Theodosius, under advisement from the pontiff. With the emperor in Constantinople and the pontiff reigning in Rome, the all-powerful church-state coalition began persecuting all who resisted her teachings.

Pagans were coerced to come to Jesus. Among those already believers, anyone refusing to switch from Sabbath to Sunday suffered persecution. Other expressions of compromised Christianity were legislated in those dark centuries that gave birth to the Holy Roman Empire.

At the turn of the millennium, faith was still a matter of force. The burning of heretics began at Orleans, France in 1022. During the great Crusades of subsequent centuries, persecution intensified.

Thomas Aquinas, the premier theologian of the middle ages, is still highly regarded today. In his classic work Summa Theologica, he urged that those who persist in rejecting church doctrine "deserve not only to be separated from the Church by excommunication, but also to be severed from the world by death." Such was the thinking of the day.

How could Christians be so cruel? Church officials believed that killing heretics saved thousands from following them into eternal torment. Even the heretics themselves might repent through fear of the flames. At least that's what church fathers hoped for as the Holy Roman Empire launched its awful Inquisitions.

Before heaping all the blame upon the medieval Roman church, it helps to know that Protestants persecuted too! They tyrannized Catholics in their territories–even non-conformist Protestants. Incredibly, Luther himself ultimately advocated persecution.

Let's remember that It was a long journey out of medieval darkness. Even the Reformers yet had much to learn and much to unlearn–as we all do today.

One of these growth areas involved baptism. The Anabaptists of the 16th century rejected Luther's practice of infant baptism. He had carried that tradition with him when leaving the Catholic church, along with other non-biblical teachings. Anabaptists, forerunners of modern Baptists, argued that nobody has the right to choose religion for another–not even parents for their children. So Baptists don't baptize babies. They dedicate little ones to God, as Mary and Joseph dedicated Baby Jesus. When children grow older, they are free to choose for themselves whether to be baptized.

Something else about baptism. The Bible says: "As soon as Jesus was baptized, He went up out of the water" (Matthew 3:16 / NIV). So He was immersed into the water, not sprinkled or poured upon. Believers in Christ are likewise "buried with Him in baptism" (Colossians 2:12).

By the way, if you have not been baptized as an adult by immersion, perhaps you might want to discuss that possibility with the friend who gave you this book.

Now, back to the intrigues of medieval Christianity. Luther's associate Melanchthon urged that Anabaptists be put to death. He predicted that their opposition to infant baptism would produce a heathen society. "Exterminate them to save the nation," he urged.

Such were the abominations of spiritual Babylon that corrupted so much of Christianity. With Catholics and Protestants both in persecution mode, Europe was a hotbed of intolerance. A whole new world needed to open up for the free exercise of faith.

## PERSECUTION IN THE NEW WORLD

Just as in Moses' day God opened a way through the Red Sea so His people could have freedom of worship, so He opened the Atlantic Ocean for the sake of religious liberty. Pilgrims sailed across on the Mayflower, escaping persecution from the Church of England. The Puritans also came across, settling what we now know as Massachusetts.

You would think they would have been happy here to enjoy their freedom and let others do the same. But no. When William Penn's band of Quakers sailed past the colony of Massachusetts, they nearly fell prey to a band of Christian pirates. Listen to this order from Cotton Mather, the famous Puritan clergyman:

"There be now at sea a ship called 'Welcome,' which has on board one hundred or more of the heretics and malignants called Quakers. . . . The General Court has given sacred orders to . . . waylay the said 'Welcome' . . . and make captive the said Penn and his ungodly crew, so that the Lord may be glorified and not mocked with the heathen worship of these people. . . . We shall not only do the Lord great good by punishing the wicked, but we shall make great good for His minister and people. Yours in the bowels of Christ, Cotton Mather."

Captivated by love! A new dimension to Christian compassion. Thank God, the preacher's persecuting pirates failed. Penn's Quakers landed safely and settled in Pennsylvania.

The Puritans not only tyrannized outsiders but oppressed their own. They spied a sea captain kissing his wife on Sunday and locked him in the stocks. The poor guy probably hadn't seen her for months. Another unfortunate fellow fell into a pond and skipped Sunday services to dry his suit. They whipped him in the name of Jesus. John Lewis and Sarah Chapman, two lovers, were brought to justice for "sitting together on the Lord's day under an apple tree in Goodman Chapman's orchard." And they weren't even doing anything, just sitting there!

Incredible legalism! And this in a land of freedom?

The Puritans with their Sunday laws missed the meaning of Sabbath rest. When Roger Williams arrived in Massachusetts in 1631, he protested their legislated legalism. Williams claimed civil magistrates had no right to enforce personal religion. The colony condemned him in 1635. He escaped arrest and fled into the snowy forest, finding refuge with the natives. "I would rather live with Christian savages," he wryly commented, "than with savage Christians."

Williams bought land from the Indians and established a new colony dedicated to religious liberty. His settlement, Providence, today is the capital of Rhode Island. Williams welcomed Jews, Catholics and Quakers as citizens in full and regular standing. Nobody suffered for their faith–or for refusing to believe. But sad to say, later leaders of Rhode Island lapsed into legalism and intolerance. And sure enough, they passed a Sunday law in 1679, requiring certain acts and forbidding others.

In that age of coerced obedience, a few had the enlightened courage to stand up for freedom. James Madison, while yet a boy in Virginia, heard a persecuted Baptist minister fearlessly preaching from the window of his prison cell. That day young Madison dedicated his life to fight for freedom of conscience. Tirelessly he toiled with Thomas Jefferson and others to secure the First Amendment in our Bill of Rights. It reads simply and majestically.: "Congress shall make no law respecting an establishment of religion, or prohibiting the free exercise thereof." Government must protect religion–but not promote it.

Our founders rejected religion by legislation. So does God! Jesus put it plainly: "Render therefore to Caesar the things that are Caesar's, and to God the things that are God's." (Matthew 22:21). Religious laws and civil laws must be kept separate. What does this mean?

God's Ten Commandments consist of two sections. The first four, including the Sabbath commandment, belong to God. They pertain to our personal relationship with Him. Civil government can't enforce matters of personal faith–the first four commandments. But the other six commandments–"Thou shalt not kill," for example–are civil laws regulating society. These statutes the state must enforce to protect human life and property. But when government intrudes upon one's personal relationship with God, problems abound.

Consider school prayer. Children should lift their hearts in prayer everywhere, including in school. Especially in school! But who should teach kids to pray? Do we want Catholic prayers? Protestant prayers? Jewish prayers? Does it matter? A while back the California state legislature selected a Buddhist chaplain. Would you like Buddhist prayers in your local school?

Who gets to choose what to pray? And who gets left out?

Some say enforcing prayer in our schools will solve their problems. But all these years, prayer has opened every session of Congress. Has government sponsored prayer overcome partisan politics?

Maybe legislated prayer isn't such a cure-all after all. Perhaps it's even a dangerous idea. Could enforcing school prayer lead to other intrusions into private religion? Perhaps even persecution again?

## FUTURE OF PERSECUTION

There is a fascinating symbol in the heart of Revelation's prophecies that appears to point to the United States. We can see there both the religious freedom we but also the impending loss of it. Notice: "Then I saw another beast coming up out of the earth, and he had two horns like a lamb and spoke like a dragon" (Revelation 13:11). A beast, by the way, simply represents a kingdom or government (see Daniel 7:17, 23).

The beast or government represented here is different from others in several ways. Previous kingdoms in Daniel and Revelation arise out of the water, which symbolizes "peoples, multitudes, nations" (Revelation 17:15)–a fitting symbol for the crowded Old World of Europe and the Middle East. Instead, this new nation springs up from the earth, which must represent new territory. Also, this new government doesn't have crowns like the others, so it's not a monarchy. Instead, it has a gentle government with two horns like a lamb.

Does this symbolize the miracle of American government, a democratic republic? Recall that colonial governments in the new world were intolerant church-state coalitions. In view of that, it is indeed amazing that when we drew up our Constitution we included a Bill of Rights that guaranteed with its First Amendment religious freedom.

A miracle indeed, this new form of government. The church-state coalition of the Holy Roman Empire violated Christ's instruction to keep separate what belongs to Caesar, the government, from what belongs to God (see Matthew 22:21). Government must protect the free exercise of religion but not promote or establish any particular belief system.

And this is what the prophecy called for: a different form of government with two lamb-like horns–the peaceful separation of two powers of church and state. And this new type of nation would emerge in a new world. What else would this be than the United States in prophecy?

How exciting! But then we notice that this gentle lamb-like government suddenly reverses course and speaks like a dragon. A nation speaks through its laws. Does this mean that America will pass legislation that would deny its democratic principles? Will we go back to the coercive ways of the Puritans, reflecting the methods of the Holy Roman Empire?

Unfortunately, some unusual and distressing events will soon occur in America. We see this in verses 12 to 14: "And he exercises all the authority of the first beast in his presence, and causes the earth and those who dwell in it to worship the first beast, whose deadly wound was healed. He performs great signs, so that he even makes fire come down from heaven on the earth in the sight of men. And he deceives those who dwell on the earth by those signs which he was granted to do in the sight of the beast, telling those who dwell on the earth to make an image to the beast who was wounded by the sword and lived."

By miracles, counterfeit miracles, our nation will lead the world to form an image to the Holy Roman Empire. What could this mean?

An image is a replica or copy of the original. The Old World power was a union of church and state, a religious system wedded to government and supported by law. This New World image to the Holy Roman Empire, being a copy of that system, must also be a union of church and state that would behave like a dragon. In other words, America will forfeit its principles of religious freedom and begin a persecution.

Incredible? Indeed. But who would expect a lamb to speak like a dragon? The Bible says America will have that drastic a change in its attitude toward religious freedom.

And did you notice that this nation has world-changing influence: "telling those who dwell on the earth" (verse 14) to reflect the principles of the old Holy Roman Empire. In our world today, only the United States has such influence, being the world's only superpower.

What could motivate America to commit its power and influence for coercion and intolerance? Perhaps some national emergency, like we've been discussing in this chapter. Remember, history shows people in crisis willingly trade liberty for security. In reaction to terrorism, perhaps. Keep in mind that the U.S. Defense Secretary warns regarding an attack of mass-destruction: "The question is no longer if this will happen, but when."

Sooner or later–and probably sooner than later–it will happen. A deadly bomb or biotoxin attack from those who are committed to bring "Death to America." And in such a holy war, anti-Islamic sentiment will inspire a firestorm of revenge on the part of NATO, led by the United States.

The Bible indicates that initially the King of the North is successful against the King of the South. Then comes an unexpected setback. A devastating terrorist attack? Because of it, the Christian West will take action against those of its own who refuse to participate in its counterfeit Christianity. It will be "enraged at the holy covenant and take action" (Daniel 11:30). This is fierce persecution against those who honor God's covenant of grace and "keep the commandments of God and the faith of Jesus" (Revelation 14:12). But Hallelujah, despite being persecuted, "the people who know their God shall be strong, and carry out great exploits" (Daniel 11:32). Amid all the opposition and satanic miracles, God will work His own wonders through His people in finishing His work on earth.

## SUNDAY LAWS

Let's recap what we've seen so far. America will face a national crisis from radical religious enemies and will react with a holy war of its own. There will be desperate and determined attempts to force the nation–and the entire Christian West–back to God. In doing so America will revert to its original roots, Colonial intolerance.

The most blatantly intolerant Colonial American legislation involved Sunday laws. And some of them packed a real sting. A Virginia law of 1610 provided that "those who violated the Sabbath or failed to attend church services, morning and afternoon, should on the first offense lose their provisions and allowance of the whole week following; for the second, lose their allowance and be publicly whipped; and for the third, suffer death."[4]

Death for violating a Sunday law! Right here in America.

Whether or not that draconian law actually was enforced, it no doubt offered powerful motivation to all who might wish to skip church on Sunday, while also warning "heretics" wanting to keep another day holy, such as the Sabbath.

Keeping Sunday has always been a trademark of the Christian West. Muslims worship on a different day, Friday. Will Sunday soon become a symbol of Christianity versus Islam? What then would happen to those who keep the Sabbath? Just as the Sabbath is in between Sunday and Friday, will those who keep God's seventh day holy find themselves caught in the struggle between the coercive Christianity and militant Islam?

It happened to the Jews. Keeping a different Sabbath has helped spark anti-Semitism through the centuries. The Holy Roman Empire has a long history of opposing the Sabbath of which Jesus proclaimed Himself Lord (see Matthew 12:8). Will Sabbath keepers in earth's final crisis likewise be persecuted?

When liberty is lost in this country it won't be because Americans have become bigots and tyrants. Rather, our freedoms will be legislated away by well-meaning Christians who know not what they do. They will sacrifice liberties trying to save the Christian West in a time of international crisis. Their goal is to regain God's favor, but they will discover too late that their efforts were on the wrong side of the Sabbath issue.

Recently, Pope John Paul II issued an encyclical urging Sunday laws in the name of social welfare. Requiring one day off seems good for society. Good for the family. Even good for saving energy. But don't believe it! Despite good intentions, Sunday laws always bring persecution.

And the Bible says history will repeat. Is the image to the beast forming right now? Zealous Christians already want to enforce the morality of the majority. What will happen next in a time of grave national danger? Let's go back to Revelation 13 and pick up where we left off:

"And he causes all, both small and great, rich and poor, free and slave, to receive a mark on their right hand or on their foreheads, and that no one may buy or sell except one who has the mark or the name of the beast, or the number of his name" (Revelation 13:16,17).

Here we have an international boycott resulting in the mark of the beast, enforced by the image to the beast. How will religious government enforce the mark? Before we explore some clues as to what the mark might be, remember God's seal, His memorial of creation. Understanding God's seal helps us identify Satan's mark.

In warning us to avoid that mark, the Bible commands us to worship Him who made heaven and earth (Revelation 14:6,7). So God's creatorship is a key issue in the final conflict. What memorial of creation has He given us? Could it be that God will use Sabbath rest to measure the loyalty of everyone who chooses to worship Him?

If Sabbath rest in Jesus represents God's seal, can we see what the mark of the beast might be? The Bible says "they have no rest day or night, who worship the beast and his image" (Revelation 14:11). No rest—no Sabbath rest!

At first glance, the matter of God's day of rest may seem trivial. But really, the Sabbath controversy isn't between one day or another. Think about it ... Are you old enough to remember when Soviet leader Nikita Kruschev visited America? He took off his shoe and pounded it on the speaker's platform. Amazing! Suppose he had demanded we Americans abandon our fourth of July and honor our country on the fifth of July instead? Would Kruschev have a right to change our day?

Suppose we had accepted his new day? What would that say about our loyalty to America?

With that in mind, let's go back for a moment to the sixteenth century and the Council of Trent. Remember that a core issue was the Protestants' insistence on using the Bible and the Bible only. Rome resisted, and here was their reason given: the church had long before shown authority to re-interpret Scripture—because influenced by tradition, it transferred the Sabbath to Sunday.

In his book Canon and Tradition, Dr. H. J. Holtzmann describes the climactic scene at the Council of Trent. Notice how the decision was reached to give tradition preference in interpreting Scripture:

"Finally ... on the eighteenth of January, 1562, all hesitation was set aside: the Archbishop of Reggio made a speech in which he openly declared that tradition stood above Scripture. The authority of the Church could therefore not be bound to the authority of the Scriptures, because the Church had changed ... the Sabbath into Sunday, not by the command of Christ, but by its own authority."

So what carried the day when all hung in the balance? It was the fact that the Roman church had actually, in effect, changed one of God's commandments, the Sabbath, on the authority of tradition. Sunday was its mark of authority.

We see, then, that the Sabbath controversy isn't over a day at all. It's over leadership. Will we obey God or yield to the beast? Whom will we trust? Where is our loyalty? The worldwide test is coming soon.

No one has the mark of the beast today. God will not permit anyone to receive that mark until the issues are out in the open. But when the issues are fully explained and all have had opportunity to understand and see the critical and final nature of the matter—then, if we deliberately choose to obey a command of men in place of a command of God, if we yield to coercion and take the easy way out—we will have marked ourselves, by our actions, as no longer loyal to God.

The mark will be there—in the forehead if we believe the propaganda of Satan. In our hand if we know it is false, but go along with it anyway. Because we can't take the pressure and the ridicule of the crowd. Or because we succumb to the economic boycott. The mark may be invisible to men. But angels will see it–and know where our loyalty lies.

God places His seal only on the forehead, the mind (see Revelation 7:3), never in the hand, for Sabbath rest isn't forced. It's free. God accepts only worship that comes from the heart and mind. Satan doesn't care how he gets his worship. If he can't win it by choice, he'll grab it by force!

As we process all we've discussed in this chapter, it's difficult to conceive of the devil working through Christian society. It's hard to see how Bible believers could ever turn to force and coercion. But then we remember the Puritans and their Sunday laws.

Ultimately, the whole earth will join forces against God's faithful remnant. There will even be a death decree.

Jesus warned: "They will put you out of the synagogues; yes, the time is coming that whoever kills you will think that he offers God service" (John 16:2). You get the picture. Persecution is not basically people who are bad trying to make other people bad, but people who are good trying to make other people good. Persecutors can be nice people who take their kids to the park to feed chipmunks. They may be filled with zeal for God, thinking it their Christian duty to suppress evil. They fail to recognize that God Himself will not force the conscience.

Racing toward the crisis hour, we cannot ignore or escape the issues at stake. And our decision must be our own. Satan would like to force his way in. Sometimes even loved ones want to enter–loved ones who do not understand. But God Himself won't violate our freedom to choose. He stands at the door of our heart and knocks. He waits for us to accept His love. Even though it may cost us jobs, our homes, our dearest earthly relationships–even our lives.

A terrifying prospect; then we recall the words of Jesus: "For whoever desires to save his life will lose it, but whoever loses his life for My sake will save it" (Luke 9:24). So "do not fear any of those things which you are about to suffer. Indeed, the devil is about to throw some of you into prison, that you may be tested, and you will have tribulation ten days. Be faithful until death, and I will give you the crown of life" (Revelation 2:10).

## TAKING A STAND

Meet Humberto Noble Alexander, a Seventh-day Adventist pastor of two small churches in New England. With his sparkling eyes and exuberant laughter, nobody would guess he spent twenty two years of his life in a loathsome Cuban dungeon, all for the sake of his faith in Christ. Somehow his faith not only survived but thrived. Noble became the unofficial pastor of an interdenominational group of worshipers.

One evening as the little group gathered for worship, Noble saw a guard quietly counting the attendees. Just as they completed singing a hymn, a soldier exploded inside and ordered all worshipers outside. "Line up!" he barked.

Everyone knew what the punishment would be–a dreaded term in the isolation chamber. They trembled in anticipation. The guard stalked up and down the line and yelled: "I see only twenty of you here. There were thirty inside. You're ten short!"

Noble was praying hard. For strength. As leader, his punishment would be the worst.

The guard kept yelling for the missing men. Meanwhile, attracted by the commotion, other prisoners drifted into the courtyard to watch. Finally the desperate guard declared, "If those ten inmates don't appear immediately, I'm going to punish the entire cell block."

Noble kept praying all the harder. Suddenly a prisoner who had never attended his meeting or shown any interest in Christianity stepped forward. "I am one of the ten men," he announced.

Then another prisoner, also not a worshiper, stepped over and joined the group. Others followed. Incredibly, as Noble kept praying, more than fifty additional prisoners declared that they had attended the meeting.

The guard's face turned red with rage and chagrin. There weren't enough isolation cells available for all these prisoners. He stomped off to consult with his supervising officer. And never came back.

After this incredible scene, many of those who took their stand began attending services and openly professed Christ as their Savior and lord. Through a crisis, they took a stand.

How about you, friend? Will you take your stand?

[1] Winfred A. Harbison and Alfred H. Kelly, *The American Constitution* (New York: W. W. Norton, 1963), p. 435.

[2] Roosevelt's programs enjoyed much smoother sailing through Congress than Lincoln's had in 1861 or Wilson's in 1917. Lower courts declined to challenge the ever-expanding federal war powers, and the Supreme Court habitually refused to overturn or even review their decisions.

[3] Samuel Walker, *In Defense of American Liberties: a History of the ACLU* (New York: Oxford University Press, 1990), p. 138.

[4] Cited in American History On-line: "The Laws of Virginia (1610-1611)."

# 9 Chapter nine

## JOURNEY TO KOINONIA

Woodstock '99. A thirtieth-year memorial of the famous festival that climaxed the psychedelic '60s. For some, perhaps, it was also a rite of passage out of the old millennium. Gen Xers brimming with anticipation and baby boomers oozing with nostalgia made the pilgrimage to their big camp meeting.

At first, things went much as expected. Lots of drugs, sex and rock 'n roll. By Sunday afternoon, though, the party was getting old. The crowd became weary of back-to-the-garden babble from blissed-out promoters who had made them pay $150 for admission. Whenever the sizzling sun incited thirst, they had to find $4 more to qualify for a few ounces of water. Porta-potties were sparse, but at least pretzels were plentiful (another $4, please).

As the weekend wound down, some guys were getting bummed out about the whole deal. They felt the urge to express themselves and release creative energies.

The opportunity came at the closing service that evening when smiling elders up front reverently distributed "peace candles"–sort of an MTV version of Holy Communion. The idea was to have everybody light somebody's candle and share the sweet spirit of love, peace and unity. Meaningful and somewhat groovy, no doubt, but a tad too sentimental for the growing gang of restless rowdies.

Seizing their peace candles, they turned them into torches. Some unhappy boomer's Mercedes love bug got burned. Other ruffians caught the spirit and set fire to the food concessions. But first, free pretzels. Then thousands cheered as giant sound towers were toppled (they must have been tired of the music by then). Soon the night was alight with flames of Waco proportions. Naked young gentlemen boogied beside the billowing orange flames, bodies glistening.

Flashbacks of Dante's Inferno.

A fire truck approached the surging mob but couldn't get though. And where were the police? About the only thing that got busted before midnight was an ATM machine!

Actually, cops were on duty at Woodstock. Two officers of the law had persuaded some young ladies to pose for pictures, blouses not required. So perhaps the police were preoccupied Sunday night, photographing the dancing Dantes.

Next morning, as smoke still swirled from the ruins, survivors wistfully loaded cars to go home. Interviewed by news reporters about the previous evening's activities, some became defensive. "It really was a friendly kind of riot," one protested. Okay, some girls in the mosh pit got groped and raped, but not too many guys were involved with that. Yea, the crowd cheered them on, but nobody meant any harm. Anyway, we gained some treasured memories to share with our grand kids thirty years from now.

The moral of the story? Be cool and don't condemn anybody. That would spoil the spirit of Woodstock.

Later that day at a press conference, the promoters seemed perplexed. Fires? Looting? Rapes? All they had wanted was to give peace a chance. And, of course, make a few bucks in the process. They were clueless about what might have gone wrong at their big love-in.

## WHAT WENT WRONG

The first thing that went wrong at Woodstock '99 was the notion that the original Woodstock was an event worth commemorating. Back in '69, its afterglow faded quickly when two of its stars died while drug overdosing: Jimi Hendrix and Janis Joplin. Later, peace activist Abbie Hoffman, who coined the term "Woodstock Nation" died his own horrible death.

Woodstock belonged to the antiwar movement of the '60s. Peace activists, flower children, and hippies felt certain they could create a peaceful, loving community. Many left mainstream society to congregate in communes that sometimes featured orgies of immorality and narcotics. But the hippies weren't all that happy; their false fellowship failed to foster the peace and love they longed for. In vain they condemned the excesses of capitalism.

On the other side of the world, communism was advancing its own secular gospel: "From each according to his ability, to each according to his need." All for one and one for all. Marx called for a revolution to form a new humanity based upon shared participation in social justice and economic prosperity. But communism never kept its promise. It caused carnage everywhere it spread and ultimately collapsed in chaos.

Meanwhile, the U. S. government of the '60s, great enemy of both communists and flower-wielding hippies, was suffering its own failed social experiment. With great fanfare President Lyndon Johnson announced his war on poverty, designed to work in tandem with the Civil Rights Act to create community. It didn't work. Several decades later, our cities are worse off. Gangs are a major source of community for young men.

When central Los Angeles was aflame in rioting and racial hatred, the question was raised: "Can't we all get along?"

Sadly, the answer is no. The hippies, communists, and the Great Society all failed. So much for the ability of secular communities to survive and thrive on this troubled planet.

Religion itself hasn't accomplished much in the way of community for its billions of devotees around the world. People who get together for religious purposes tend to cause big trouble. In India, Hindus and Muslims gather in mobs to destroy each other's worship houses. In the Middle East and Africa, radical Muslims congregate in terrorist cell groups plotting mayhem. Right wing Jewish settlement communities on the West Bank are both the perpetrators and victims of violence. People who form communities in God's name too often end up hurting other people.

Even so-called Christianity has failed to foster the building of community. In the Balkans, "faith" fuels the fire of fratricide. In Ireland, Protestant and Catholic communities still have a difficult time not bombing each other's funerals. In Latin America, the so-called liberation movement betrayed its name. In North America, popular televangelists became legends for preaching love while living in lust.

Will it ever happen? Will God someday have a community on earth that showcases His principles of love, fellowship and integrity?

## BACK TO EDEN

He has been trying for a long time. Let's go back in the garden of Eden, where God created the first human being. He declared it wasn't good to leave Adam lonely, so He gave him a wife. Together they formed a community of oneness. Beyond the marriage relationship,

God intended that all humanity through Adam would comprise the community of His children. This unity of fellowship is reflected in the very nature of the Creator, where three separate, eternal Persons comprise the corporate unit of the Godhead (see Genesis 1:1-3; Colossians 2:9,10).

When sin slithered into this planet, it immediately poisoned humanity's community relationship. Man and woman turned on each other (see Genesis 3:12). They also severed their relationship with God, hiding from His presence (verse 8). Heartbroken at the alienation caused by sin, God took action to restore the oneness given humanity at creation. The Word became flesh to live among us and reestablish community–not just our individual relationship with Him but also to form a corporate body known as the church, replacing the original community of humanity lost when Adam sinned.

Community was always at the heart of Christ's ministry. The night before He died, Jesus gathered his band of disciples and washed their feet. Why? To bond them in community. Then He poured out His soul in prayer to His Father that all of us would be a united body of believers (see John 17).

After that prayer, Jesus led His disciples down the moonlit trail to the garden of Gethsemane. With the burden of our sin staggering His soul, He felt His eternal oneness with the Father breaking apart. It had to happen for Him to be our Savior. He had to pick up where Adam failed, suffering in Himself the separation from community with God that resulted from our sin.

Two pieces of wood comprised the cross of our salvation. On the vertical beam the body of Jesus linked heaven above with earth below, restoring fallen humanity's community with God. On the horizontal beam His arms stretched wide to unite us in community with one another. At the point where those cross beams met, the heart of Jesus broke and He died. In doing that He "abolished in His flesh the enmity, . . . so as to create in Himself one new man from the two, thus making peace" (Ephesians 2:15).

When Jesus rose in triumph from the grave, He activated this new humanity in which all believers participate by faith. In Christ we belong to an entirely new human race known as the church. "We, being many, are one body in Christ, and individually members of one another" (Romans 12:5). While baptism is a once-in-a-lifetime symbol of our oneness in Christ, the Communion service is an ongoing celebration of that oneness (see 1 Corinthians 10:16,17).

Picture again Christ's physical body hanging on the cross. The meeting point of those two beams of wood was the physical spot where His heart broke—and also the bonding place of all redeemed humanity. Black or white, male or female, rich or poor; all now have oneness in Christ Jesus. This community of believers is the church, the body of Christ, "in whom you also are being built together for a dwelling place of God in the Spirit" (Ephesians 2:22).

Our oneness in the Spirit abolishes forever all the devil's "isms." Racism. Chauvinism. Materialism. Exclusivism. Each of those enemies of community will melt like ice in the springtime sun when we appreciate and activate our oneness in Jesus. Meanwhile, as those evil "isms" still reside around us—and within us—the question confronts us: Is genuine, unpolluted fellowship an impossible fantasy?

No. For a brief time in early Christianity, God's people did share true community in Christ. Here's an intriguing description of daily life among them:

"And they continued steadfastly in the apostles' doctrine and fellowship, in the breaking of bread, and in prayers. . . . Now all who believed were together, and had all things in common, and sold their possessions and goods, and divided them among all, as anyone had need. So continuing daily with one accord in the temple, and breaking bread from house to house, they ate their food with gladness and simplicity of heart, praising God and having favor with all the people. And the Lord added to the church daily those who were being saved" (Acts 2:42-47).

This community had it all—unselfishness, camaraderie, tremendous joy, and daily church growth. The key word in that passage is fellowship, translated from the fascinating Greek word koinonia (pronounced koy-noh-nee'-ah). Notice its different uses throughout the New Testament. First, in describing our relationship with the Lord: "God is faithful, by whom you were called into the fellowship [koinonia] of His Son, Jesus Christ our Lord" (1 Corinthians 1:9). Also included is our community with each other: "That which we have seen and heard we declare to you, that you also may have fellowship [koinonia] with us; and truly our fellowship [koinonia] is with the Father and with His Son Jesus Christ" (1 John 1:3).

Week by week the Sabbath offers koinonia, fellowship with God and with each other. Shunning secular business on the seventh day is not for the sake of proving anything or racking up individual points with God. We join with our families and friends in celebrating communally the accomplishments of Jesus Christ. So Sabbath rest in Jesus is a festival of koinonia.

## WHERE IS THAT CHURCH?

Is there a church here and now that offers true community in Christ–including the opportunity for Sabbath koinonia?

Here is the story of one church family. It originated within a world-wide awakening of interest in Christ's second coming. In England, several hundred ministers began preaching that Jesus was coming soon. The message also circulated in South America, Europe, Asia and parts of Africa. Joseph Wolff, known as "missionary to the world," even proclaimed the soon return of Jesus, upon invitation, before the assembled Congress of the United States.

The Adventist message startled Christianity out of its slumbers. News of Christ's second coming had become a neglected truth–in sad contrast to the days of early Christianity when it was a burning obsession. In fact, the apostle Paul proclaimed Christ's return to be the "blessed hope" (Titus 2:13). As the centuries passed, however, the second advent of Jesus was nearly forgotten. It joined a long list of neglected truths.

Having forsaken God's truth, the church experienced internal trauma–just as the Bible predicted (see Acts 20:28-30). Truth would suffer from perversity. In the pages of this book we've seen how that happened. But God was not content to leave His light buried under a bushel of medieval darkness. Five hundred years ago He raised up reformers to champion forgotten truth. Martin Luther restored the heartbeat of Christianity, that good news about salvation being a free gift through the life, death, and resurrection of Jesus Christ. And so the Reformation began–but it was not finished by the Lutherans in the 16th century. Actually, it would be asking too much that all of the truths hidden for so long could be recovered immediately. Restoring the ancient biblical faith was a time-consuming process.

Luther's re-discovery of the gospel brought us the Lutheran church. But he did not clearly see the importance of certain other truths, such as baptism by immersion. The Anabaptists approached leading Protestant scholars and urged them to accept this new light. We might have hoped they would, but they didn't. So we have our Baptist church today. And when other truths came through Wesley, the established churches turned him down. This made the Methodist church necessary. The story goes on and on.

You see the problem. It's the human tendency to depend upon past beliefs, drawing a circle around our beliefs and calling it a creed. These historic creeds helped secure the foundation of Christianity but failed to make provision for additional light. As further truths have been recovered, other movements have sprung into existence, each championing newly re-discovered light. That's why we have so many denominations today.

By the early 1840s, the world was ripe for the movement that restored the neglected truth of Christ's second coming. Society, caught up with the dawning Industrial Revolution, was looking for a future in human accomplishment. Churches of the time typically taught that conditions on earth would improve and introduce a golden era of peace. No wonder most resisted the news that Christ would come soon and interrupt the good life on this earth. Many "Adventists," as those who believed in the soon coming of Christ were called, were evicted from their own churches. Others left on their own to join with fellow believers who were looking for the Lord's immediate return.

William Miller and his followers expected Christ to come in 1844, based upon the 2,300-year time prophecy of Daniel chapters 8 and 9. When that date passed without the appearance of Jesus, disappointment crushed the believers. Imagine how they felt. Many lost courage and forfeited their faith. Others, convinced that God remained with them, continued their study of the Bible.

They came across something that brought great comfort and relief. Long ago another religious movement had suffered a great disappointment–the Christian church itself. When Jesus was crucified, His disciples felt disappointed and defeated. With the scoffing of unbelievers ringing in their ears, they faltered in their faith.

Even though the disciples' expectations regarding their Messiah had failed, God remained with them. He had been leading them all along and planned a bright future for their movement. Likewise, the nineteenth century Adventists had been led by God during their great disappointment. Soon additional light came to an Adventist group in New England through a Seventh-day Baptist young woman. She referred them to the fourth commandment, pointing out that God had never withdrawn Sabbath rest from His people. True, the Sabbath had been nearly forgotten during the dark centuries. Yet the seventh day remains an eternal memorial of the work of Jesus. Adventists cherished this unexpected gem of neglected truth, just as they welcomed the other truths recovered by various denominations since the Protestant Reformation.

Have you ever wondered how those various denominations chose their names? Some named themselves according to their governing structure. "Episcopalian," for example, means that bishops have supreme authority in the church. And "Congregational" shows that local congregations make decisions for themselves.

Other churches are named for their founders, like the Lutherans. Then there are churches that take their name from important truths they teach. Such as the Baptists, named after their belief in the biblical form of baptism. Of course, all Christians who are baptized by immersion are Baptists in the general sense. And those who belong to that body of believers are Baptists in the specific sense.

Now, let's apply what we've been studying personally. If you believe in Christ's second advent, you can consider yourself an Adventist, in a general sense. Seventh-day Adventists take their name from two basic truths about Jesus. "Adventist" refers to the fact that Jesus is coming soon. "Seventh-day" lets people know they observe the day which honors Christ as Creator and Redeemer. So the name Seventh-day Adventist proclaims truth about Jesus, neglected truth, needed to be recovered to complete the Reformation.

For the last one hundred fifty years, Adventist believers have proclaimed these last messages of warning in the book of Revelation.

Since the 1860's, when the Seventh-day Adventist Church was officially organized, congregations have sprung up in nearly two hundred countries around the world. Did you know that Adventists are now among the fastest growing Christian groups? More than two thousand believers every day are joining this family of believers. World membership is more than ten million.

Along with proclaiming Bible truth, Seventh-day Adventists have always cared about the physical and social needs of people. They operate 460 hospitals and clinics around the globe. As a community service, they also offer stop-smoking and weight-loss seminars, along with classes on meatless cooking.

Through the Adventist Development and Relief Agency (ADRA), the church responds immediately to disasters anywhere in the world with clothing, food and medical supplies. Many local congregations operate Community Service Centers, where volunteers minister to the hungry and homeless.

Adventists believe in Christian education, sponsoring some five thousand elementary and secondary schools—the largest Protestant parochial school system in the world—plus more than ninety colleges and universities. They also proclaim the gospel through the radio broadcast "Voice of Prophecy" and telecasts such as "It Is Written" and "Faith for Today." To the watching audience of African-Americans, Adventists offer "Breath of Life." And reaching out to Hispanic Americans is the broadcast, "La Voz de la Esperanza" (The Voice of Hope). All these ministries are headquartered at the Adventist Media Center in California.

What do you think of the Seventh-day Adventist Church so far? Do you find yourself drawn to this family of believers? There are solid reasons why so many dedicated Christians are joining this fellowship. They realize that Adventists have gathered together neglected gems of light, truth originally taught by the apostles and recovered by the reformers. The faith in Jesus of the Lutherans. The baptism by immersion of the Baptists. The interest in spiritual growth and Spirit-filled living of the Methodists and Charismatics. The respect for morality of the Catholics. The seventh-day Sabbath championed by our Jewish ancestors and cherished by Jesus and the apostles. All of these truths Seventh-day Adventists have brought together in one body of belief.

Perhaps you are thinking, "I can see how God has led the Seventh-day Adventist Church, but I'm happy in my own church. The Lord has blessed me there and I don't want to leave it!"

Surely the Lord has been leading you along. But now is it possible He has further light for you to follow? At your present church, do you hear the truth about Jesus Christ being Lord of the Sabbath? Do they worship on the seventh day as God commands? In case the church you have been attending can't accommodate your new convictions, there is one that will meet that need. And you can even experience worship there this coming Sabbath!

Most Adventist churches in North America offer a Saturday morning worship hour at 11:00. Often a fellowship lunch follows, if you want to stay around and sample some of that delicious koinonia we've been talking about! Ask about Sabbath school classes for both adults and children, which typically are scheduled just before weekly worship. Your local church family probably sponsors other activities through the week for both adults and children. In everything Adventists do, guests are always welcome. So you'll meet others just like yourself who are checking things out.

When visiting your local Adventist church family, you'll quickly discover we're not perfect. Any group of people has its share of problems! The difference is that here is one place where you won't have to compromise your convictions about truth. Here is somewhere you can grow in your understanding of God's Word and worship in the full expression of your faith. You'll probably also find a lot of love. And you'll meet new friends whom God has led on the same journey toward truth that you have traveled while reading this book.

What a heritage God has in store for us today, highlighting the vital truths recovered by the great Reformers–and now in the final phase of the Reformation, still rediscovering truth. Shouldn't we all, whatever our denomination may be, keep following advancing light? This is God's challenge to the alert, thinking Christian.

More than ten million around the world are Adventists, with more than two thousand joining every day. Should you be among them?

Something to think about, and pray about too. You might discuss any questions you have with the friend who shared this book with you.

## TRUTH IS THE TEST

Quite possibly in these pages you've become acquainted with new truth. God is stretching you out of your comfort zone into your courageous zone. But suppose loved ones object to what God has been teaching you. What then? Should you give up the truth?

It all comes down to this: Who is most important in our lives? Jesus said, "He who loves father or mother more than Me is not worthy of Me. And he who loves son or daughter more than Me is not worthy of Me. And he who does not take his cross and follow after Me is not worthy of Me. He who finds his life will lose it, and he who loses his life for My sake will find it" (Matthew 10:37-39).

Tough words, tough love from Jesus, our friend, our Savior—and the Lord of the Sabbath. He is the one who created us. He is the one who died for us. To Him above all others we owe our loyalty and obedience. Loved ones just need to know that first and foremost, we are disciples of Jesus. He is number one in our lives. It's our privilege and responsibility to follow wherever He leads us by the truths of His Word.

Perhaps for the time being, people you love may not understand how God is leading you. But if you trust God anyway and step out in obedience to His Word, they will learn to adjust to your new convictions. Anyone who truly loves you will learn to respect your right and your need to follow the Lord. It really comes down to a matter of religious liberty, freedom of conscience.hg

Meanwhile, if your faith is tested in obeying Bible truth, you can thank God for this opportunity to prepare for earth's final crisis. During that time of trouble, each soul will be tested to the limit. You can settle it here and now that come what may, you will be faithful to your God.

Faithful indeed, but not by yourself or in your own strength! He promises: "Fear not, for I am with you; be not dismayed, for I am your God. I will strengthen you, yes, I will help you, ... For I, the

Lord your God, will hold your right hand, saying to you, 'Fear not, I will help you'" (Isaiah 41:10,13).

Remember the words of Jesus: "Do not fear any of those things which you are about to suffer. Indeed, the devil is about to throw some of you into prison, that you may be tested, ... Be faithful until death, and I will give you the crown of life" (Revelation 2:10).

The best day of your life will be happening soon. You will look up in the sky and see Jesus coming in all His glory, eager to take you home to heaven. His smile of appreciation and welcome for you will make everything you've endured for Him more than worth it all.

So then, come Lord Jesus!